Jacques Pépin

More Fast Food My Way

Jacques Pépin

More Fast Food My Way

Photographs by Tom Hopkins

Houghton Mifflin Company

Boston · New York

2008

ISBN-13: 978-0-618-14233-0
ISBN-10: 0-618-14233-9

Book design by Ralph Fowler
Food styling by Jacques Pépin

Printed in the United States of America

To Jean-Claude,

my alter ego in the kitchen,

a most generous spirit always eager

to help with a smile.

CONTENTS

INTRODUCTION

When I wrote *Fast Food My Way,* I hoped that many of my friends would prepare my recipes and feel comfortable cooking this way. It turned out better than I had expected and now more people cook from this book than any other of the twenty or so books that I have written in the last thirty years. Friends, family, neighbors, students, and colleagues alike tell me how happily surprised they are by the results, especially given the minimal investment of time. It amazes many cooks that a few simple and uncomplicated steps can produce such great dishes, and they often say, "That's it!? That's all there is to it?" Yes, simplicity was one of the main assets of *Fast Food My Way,* and the same is true of *More Fast Food My Way:* simplicity of thinking, techniques, ingredients, combinations, and presentation.

The best, freshest ingredients are essential as well for this "fast food," even though great use is made in the book of the pantry and canned food. This is not a paradox: your canned sardines will be better served on a bed of the freshest baby arugula with a sprinkling of great olives, and a can of cannellini beans that you have transformed into a soup will be accented and improved with great sausage, fresh herbs, mild onion, and roasted croutons from an earthy country bread. Using the supermarket the right way, you can buy good-quality partially cooked or prepared food and make that food personal with a few additions or changes. It's a gratifying way to cook and it makes you feel that you have created something. This is the easiest of my cookbooks for beginners, for people afraid to cook, for people pressed for time or limited by a poorly stocked supermarket or by a family of finicky eaters, or for anyone who wants great food quickly.

When I think about "fast food" cooking, I realize that I have always cooked this way. My mother did so and so occasionally do my professional chef friends. We all have moments when, pressed by time, we'll use a can of tuna and a tomato to make a first course or we'll transform frozen raspberries into a scrumptious dessert in minutes. It's a question of choosing the right recipes. On a leisurely weekend I may take my time making long-simmering stocks, puff pastry, and slow-cooked stews. A couple of days later, I may be stuck in traffic, come home late, and be hungry and short of time, so I'll concoct a few fast dishes with what is available in my pantry and fridge—often with as much success as a long-planned, time-consuming meal. These recipes are as much a part of my culinary past and as much a part of my cuisine as are the more complex, longer-to-make recipes from my other books.

In a restaurant, the food is ready in minutes because of thorough beforehand preparation. The work is always divided into two parts, the preparation (called the *mise en place*) and the mealtime finishing touches at the stove (called *le service*). The prep cook bones the chicken, fillets the fish, minces the shallots, slices the mushrooms, cleans the spinach, peels the tomatoes, and chops the herbs ahead, all to be ready for mealtime. Then, if a customer orders a fish dish, it takes the cook at the

stove only seconds to combine the fish with presliced mushrooms, chopped shallots, peeled tomatoes, and wine, and a couple of minutes to cook the dish and finish it with a pat of butter and fresh herbs.

The supermarket is my modest, efficient prep cook, there specifically to make my life easier. At my disposal are prewashed baby greens and spinach, presliced mushrooms, skinless and boneless chicken breasts and thighs, fish fillets, shelled peas and beans, precooked beets, precleaned vegetables for soup, and much more. At the deli counter, many varieties of olives, marinated mushrooms, pimientos, and all kinds of grated, crumbled, or sliced cheeses stand ready to be used in salads or as garnishes. I find rolled sushi, raw stuffed roasts of veal, stuffed chickens, and marinated ribs. As I see the products, recipes pop into my head. I can make rotisserie chickens my own by cutting them up and placing them on a bed of Boston lettuce sprinkled with sautéed shallots, garlic, and herbs (see page 21).

Good equipment is important as well. I use a pressure cooker to make a fast delicious curry of lamb (page 118) and a spicy chili con carne (page 106). A food processor, a grater, sharp knives, nonstick pans, and rubber spatulas are as essential as are great olive oil, eggs, chicken stock, and breads, along with the freshest vegetables and salad greens and superb nuts, olives, and cheeses.

A few changes in your habits can save a lot of time. Peel vegetables directly into the sink or the garbage can. Line trays with aluminum foil to save time on washing and keep using the same pot when you cook, rinsing it quickly between uses and filling it with water when you are finished with it. Cook in attractive vessels, like a red cast-iron Dutch oven that you can bring directly from the stove to the table. If using a food processor more than once—let's say to make bread crumbs and a puree of peas—start with the crumbs, so you don't have to wash the bowl between uses.

This cuisine is the answer when guests invited for drinks are still lingering two hours later at dinnertime. Then is the time to survey the pantry and the refrigerator to see what you can cook with a minimum of effort. More than anything else, you may be surprised at how elegant and easy this type of entertaining can be. Your "fast food" will be different from mine, because along the way you'll discover your own shortcuts and your own special style that you can apply to the dishes in this book to give them your personal stamp.

Happy, easy, and elegant cooking!

MINUTE RECIPES

SEASONED OLIVES

The deli at my supermarket offers six different kinds of olives and I like to combine and season some of the pitted ones to make my own mixture. My favorite varieties are kalamata, oil-cured, and small green olives. These are excellent with drinks.

To 1 cup mixed pitted olives, add 1 tablespoon lemon zest, about 2 teaspoons fresh lemon juice, 2 tablespoons extra-virgin olive oil, and 1 teaspoon *each* shredded fresh oregano and fresh sage. Mix well and warm for about 30 seconds in a microwave oven to develop the flavor.

MAKES ABOUT 1 CUP

CHEESE BALLS WITH PIGNOLI NUTS

I love cheese and always buy more than I consume. Through the years, I have worked out a number of recipes to use leftover cheese, so I don't have to feel guilty about it spoiling. This appetizer is best done with soft cheeses, like fontina, Camembert, blue, St. Albray, or Reblochon. Pear and dried cranberries lend a little sweetness and the toasted pignoli nuts add richness and texture—a perfect combination.

Spread about ¾ cup pignoli nuts on a baking sheet. Bake in a preheated 400-degree oven for 6 to 8 minutes, or until lightly browned. Set aside to cool. Remove any skin or mold from enough soft cheese—one variety or a mixture of those listed above or others—to yield 1 cup. Break into 1-inch pieces. Put the cheese in a food processor with ½ cup 1-inch pieces of peeled pear or apple, 2 tablespoons dried cranberries, and ¼ teaspoon *each* salt and freshly ground black pepper. Process until the mixture is still chunky but is well combined and beginning to stick together. Divide into 18 small portions of about 2 teaspoons each. Shape into small balls. Roll in the toasted pignoli nuts to coat. Refrigerate until serving time.

MAKES 18 SMALL CHEESE BALLS

BEET, STILTON, APPLE, AND NUT SALAD

This classic salad makes an elegant and tasty first course for a dinner or a great lunch main dish. I simplify the preparation by using sliced canned beets.

Drain the juice from a 1-pound can of sliced beets. Divide the slices among four plates, allotting 4 or 5 slices per plate. Mix together in a bowl ¾ cup coarsely chopped white mushrooms, about 1 cup peeled and coarsely chopped apple, ½ cup broken walnut pieces, and ½ cup crumbled Stilton cheese. Add 3 tablespoons mayonnaise and salt and freshly ground black pepper to taste and mix well. Spoon a good dollop of the mixture into the middle of the sliced beets on the plates and sprinkle on 1 teaspoon of chopped fresh chives. Serve.

4 SERVINGS

CRABMEAT HORSERADISH SALAD

I can buy good-quality, refrigerated, canned Maryland crabmeat for a reasonable price at my supermarket. I use it for crab cakes and salad, as well as serving it in soups, but I particularly like it for crabmeat cocktail, which I serve in stemmed glasses lined with the small, white, crunchy inside leaves of Boston lettuce.

Line four wide-mouthed glasses, plates, or glass bowls with Boston lettuce leaves. Mix together in a small bowl ⅓ cup ketchup, 1½ teaspoons fresh lemon juice, 1 tablespoon grated horseradish (I make my own, but you can use store-bought), and a dash each of salt and Tabasco hot pepper sauce. Spoon ⅓ to ½ cup crabmeat into the center of the salad greens on each plate. Coat the crab with the horseradish sauce. Serve cold with flatbread wedges or breadsticks.

4 SERVINGS

GOAT CHEESE TOASTS

Goat cheese toasts make excellent hors d'oeuvres or garnishes for a salad. I like the small Bûcheron goat cheese, which is about 1¾ inches in diameter, or any other soft, creamy, and mild goat cheese of about the same size. Montrachet is also a very good imported chèvre, or goat cheese. Combining the cheese with a little herbes de Provence or Italian seasoning and some slivered garlic adds complexity. The toasts can be assembled and toasted at the last minute.

Preheat the broiler. Cut as many ¼-inch slices from a baguette as you need for serving. Arrange the slices side by side on a baking sheet. Cut enough ¼-inch-thick slices from a tubelike container of goat cheese (dental floss is good for slicing the cheese) for each of the bread rounds. Press a slice of cheese on each slice of bread, taking care to cover the entire surface of the bread so it doesn't burn under the broiler. Sprinkle a small amount of herbes de Provence on each toast and a bit of freshly ground black pepper. Using a vegetable peeler, remove thin slices from a large peeled garlic clove and press 1 sliver in the center of the cheese on each toast. Sprinkle each toast with a few drops of olive oil. Slide the toasts under the broiler, so they are 4 to 5 inches from the heat source, for about 2 minutes, or until the tops are bubbly, hot, and lightly browned. Arrange the toasts on a serving platter. Cool for about 5 minutes before serving.

CURED HERRING STARTER

This is a winner when guests drop by unexpectedly.

Drain a 12-ounce jar of herring in white wine. Combine in a bowl with 1 tablespoon *each* drained capers and bottled horseradish, ½ cup peeled and diced (¼-inch) cucumber, and ½ cup peeled and diced (½-inch) apple. Add a good dash of salt and Tabasco hot pepper sauce and ¼ cup sour cream. Toss with 4 cups mesclun salad greens. Serve on plates or in martini glasses.

4 SERVINGS

RADISH TOASTS

The conventional way to eat radishes in France is to split them partially open and insert a small piece of butter in the opening, then to dip the top of the radish lightly in coarse salt and enjoy it with a piece of crunchy baguette. I sometimes prepare a variation of this French recipe.

Cut a baguette into thin slices about ⅜ inch thick. Cover each slice lavishly with unsalted butter. Thinly slice several radishes horizontally (a vegetable peeler is good for this) and cover the butter with overlapping slices of radish. Sprinkle a little fleur de sel on top and enjoy with drinks.

6 TO 8 SERVINGS

SPANISH TOMATO BREAD AND SERRANO HAM OR PROSCIUTTO

I first enjoyed a dish similar to this at the Guggenheim Museum designed by Frank Gehry in Bilbao, Spain. A Rioja red wine is best with this appetizer.

Rub 4 well-toasted slices of crusty, country-style bread with a large garlic clove. Halve a very ripe tomato and press out the seeds and juice. Rub the halved tomato vigorously on the toasted bread slices to coat the bread with the "pureed" tomato flesh. (Do not make these more than 1 hour ahead, or the tomato will make the toast soggy.) Sprinkle on a little of your best olive oil and a dash of coarse salt, like fleur de sel. Serve the toasts with a couple of slices of serrano ham, prosciutto, or chorizo sausage.

4 SERVINGS

MINI CROQUES-MONSIEUR

For these tidbits, I use good Jarlsberg, Gruyère, Beaufort, or Comté cheese and the best boiled ham that I can find at my market. The sandwiches can be prepared ahead and baked as needed for a large party or wedding reception.

Arrange **2 thick slices white bread** next to one another on the counter and cover 1 slice completely with **slices of cheese**. Add **1 slice ham** to cover the cheese and then add another layer of **cheese and ham** before finishing with the other slice of bread. Spread about **1 teaspoon butter** on each side of the sandwich and arrange it on a foil-lined cookie sheet. Bake in a preheated 375-degree oven for about 12 minutes, or until the croque-monsieur is brown and crusty on both sides. Cool for about 5 minutes. Trim off the crust if you like and cut into 6 small rectangles. Serve hot with toothpicks.

MAKES 6 MINI SANDWICHES

RED PEPPER DIP

Roasted red peppers are sold at the deli counter. I transform them into a fast dip to enjoy with cocktails.

Cut enough **roasted red bell pepper** into 1-inch pieces to make 1 cup. Transfer to a food processor. Add **2 tablespoons sunflower seeds** or **pumpkin seeds**, **¼ cup cream cheese**, **1 tablespoon olive oil**, and **¼ teaspoon each salt** and **freshly ground black pepper**. Process until smooth. Serve with **crunchy breadsticks**.

MAKES ABOUT 1½ CUPS

BASIL AND CHEESE DIP

Put about 3 cups (lightly packed) washed basil leaves in a plastic bag or glass bowl with a cover. Microwave for about 30 seconds. Dump the hot basil from the bag into a blender. Add ¼ cup extra-virgin olive oil, ¼ cup cool water, ¼ cup grated Parmesan cheese, ½ teaspoon salt, and ¼ teaspoon freshly ground black pepper. Process until finely pureed. (As a variation, you can add about ½ cup diced (¼-inch) Gruyère cheese and stir well.) Serve with bagel chips, Melba Toast (page 23), or potato chips. The dip stays brilliant green and keeps for a few days in the refrigerator.

MAKES ABOUT 1 CUP

SAVORY ICEBERG CUPS

I fill everything from tortillas to wonton skins to phyllo with cheese, ham, salad, olives, sausage, or meatballs. For a light, crunchy, delicate, low-calorie wrap, I sometimes use the center leaves of iceberg lettuce, which are shaped like cups and are easy to fill, wrap, and eat.

From 1 head iceberg lettuce, remove 8 center leaves, each about the size of your cupped hands held together. Arrange them side by side on a platter. In a bowl, mix together 1 cup crumbled (½-inch pieces) feta cheese, 1 cup (½-inch pieces) drained oil-packed sun-dried tomatoes, 1 cup (½-inch pieces) chopped red bell pepper or pimiento, 1 cup pitted spicy green olives, whole if small or cut into ½-inch pieces, and 1 teaspoon chopped garlic. Add 2 tablespoons fresh lemon juice, ¼ cup olive oil, 1 tablespoon chopped fresh tarragon, and ¾ teaspoon each salt and freshly ground black pepper and mix well. Divide among the iceberg lettuce cups. Wrap the cups to enclose the filling, if you like, or serve as is.

MAKES 8 HORS D'OEUVRE WRAPS

BUTTER BEAN CANAPÉS

I love beans and the big butter beans *(habas grandes)* available in cans at the supermarket are well suited for these canapés. The bean mixture also makes a great first-course salad or meat accompaniment. If made up to 3 hours ahead, the bread will, for the better, soak up the juices from the beans.

Mix together in a bowl 1 can (15.5 ounces) drained butter beans (large white beans), 1 tablespoon Dijon mustard, 2 tablespoons fresh lemon juice, 3 tablespoons chopped onion, 2 tablespoons chopped fresh parsley or chives, 1 teaspoon chopped garlic, 3 tablespoons extra-virgin olive oil, and ½ teaspoon *each* salt and freshly ground black pepper. Cut twelve ⅓-inch-thick slices from a baguette. Mound the bean mixture on the bread slices. Serve.

MAKES ABOUT 3 DOZEN

CURED SALMON MORSELS

Gravlax is one of my favorite hors d'oeuvres, and I usually present it on buttered bread or cucumber slices. One day when I was slicing salmon, I decided to cut some of it into small cubes, quickly cure them, and serve them on toothpicks. These only take a minute to prepare. The fresher the salmon, the more outstanding the finished morsels.

Cut about 8 ounces cleaned salmon into 1-inch cubes. Sprinkle with about ¾ teaspoon salt, ½ teaspoon sugar, and ½ teaspoon freshly ground black pepper. Toss the cubes together in a small bowl and let cure for about 10 minutes. Meanwhile, finely chop some fresh herbs (chives, tarragon, and parsley). Toss the salmon pieces with the herbs to coat them well and arrange them on a serving plate. Stick a toothpick in each cube. Sprinkle with the best extra-virgin olive oil and serve.

MAKES ABOUT 30 PIECES

FRIED CAPERS

For an unusual cocktail accompaniment, I like to deep-fry capers. Although small capers are preferred for most recipes, the largest capers available are the best for deep-frying. Crunchy and nutty, these will surprise and delight your guests.

Drain a **3- to 4-ounce jar large capers** in a sieve. Rinse well under cool tap water to remove excess salt. Dry thoroughly on paper towels. Heat **½ to 1 inch canola** or **safflower oil** to about 350 degrees in a skillet. Add the capers and cook for about 2 minutes, moving them around gently with a slotted spoon. They should be light brown and dry. Drain on paper towels and when cool enough to handle, transfer to a serving bowl.

MAKES ABOUT ½ CUP

SWEET CRISP BACON

I learned how to cook bacon in a microwave oven from my wife and I now never cook it any other way. It's easy and fast and crisps the bacon uniformly. There can be variations in timing from one microwave to another, but regular bacon generally cooks in about 4 minutes and thicker slices require up to 6 minutes. Cook the thick slices for 4 minutes initially and then check them every 30 seconds or so and continue until the bacon is cooked to your liking. Choose as lean a bacon as you can find. I prefer thick-sliced bacon. Brushing the top of the slices with maple syrup or honey imparts a delicious taste.

Arrange **4 bacon slices** side by side in one layer on a corrugated microwave tray. Brush with **2 teaspoons maple syrup**, turn, and brush on the other side with **2 teaspoons more syrup**. Cover loosely with a sheet of paper towel and microwave on high for 4 minutes. Check, cook for another 30 seconds, and then check again. Continue cooking, checking every 30 seconds, until the bacon is well crisped (about 6 minutes total).

4 SERVINGS

ASIAN CHICKEN LIVERS

These livers, which are poached and served in a hot sauce, are a fabulous appetizer. The sauce, which can be made ahead, is also good with steamed fish, as a seasoning for salad, or sprinkled over steamed vegetables. The livers take only about 2 minutes to cook.

Cut about **5 chicken livers** in half. Remove and discard any sinew that was connecting the halves. Cut the halves in half again. Bring a pot of salted water to a boil. Put the liver pieces in a sieve. Meanwhile, in a bowl large enough to accommodate the livers, mix **2 tablespoons dark soy sauce** with **1 teaspoon sugar, 1 teaspoon chopped garlic, 2 teaspoons balsamic vinegar, 1½ tablespoons toasted sesame oil, 2 tablespoons water,** and **1 tablespoon finely chopped fresh cilantro**. When the water in the pot is boiling, lower the sieve containing the liver pieces into the water and cook for about 2 minutes. The water will have barely come back to a boil. Remove the livers; they should be pink inside. Add to the bowl of sauce and mix well. Serve with chopsticks or forks.

4 TO 6 SERVINGS (20 PIECES)

ANCHOVY SPREAD

This is an appetizer for anchovy aficionados. My wife adores this spread on pasta, toast or, as I suggest here, on cheese.

Put the contents of a **2-ounce can of anchovies** in a food processor or mini chopper. Add **¼ cup whole almonds, 1 garlic clove, 1 washed and quartered white mushroom, ¾ cup diced (½-inch) country bread** (preferably from a day-or-two-old loaf), and **3 tablespoons best-quality olive oil**. Process until the mixture is coarsely chopped. Cut ¼-inch-thick slices from a firm cheese like **Gruyère, Manchego, or provolone**. Cut the slices into 1-inch squares. Spoon about 1 teaspoon of the anchovy spread on each square of cheese, garnish with **sliced almonds**, and serve.

MAKES ABOUT 20 SMALL CANAPÉS

EGGS AND ANCHOVIES

This delicious first course was a favorite at my mother's restaurant in Lyon when I was a teenager. Since I usually have all the garnishes in my refrigerator, nothing could be easier to prepare, but the eggs have to be cooked properly.

Lower 4 large eggs into boiling water to cover, bring the water back to a very low boil, and boil gently for 9 minutes. Pour out the hot water and shake the pan to crack the eggshells. Fill the pan with cold water and ice and let the eggs cool thoroughly. Shell the eggs and halve them lengthwise. Place 2 halved eggs on each of two plates or on a platter. In a small bowl, whisk together until smooth 3 tablespoons mayonnaise, 1 tablespoon water, 1 tablespoon ketchup, and a good dash of Tabasco hot pepper sauce. Coat the eggs with the sauce. Place 1 anchovy fillet on top of each halved egg. Sprinkle on a few capers. Divide about 1 tablespoon chopped red onion among the four plates. Serve.

2 SERVINGS

SURIMI SALAD ON GREENS

Surimi—imitation crabmeat—is usually made with pollock or scrod. It comes vacuum-packed and I keep a package of it in my refrigerator for a fast first course or last-minute hors d'oeuvre.

In a bowl, combine about 2 cups (1-inch pieces) surimi, 2 tablespoons mayonnaise, 2 tablespoons sour cream, 3 tablespoons minced scallions, 1½ tablespoons chopped shallot or onion, 2 tablespoons fresh lemon juice, ¼ teaspoon salt, and a good dash Tabasco hot pepper sauce. Divide about 2 cups mesclun salad greens among four plates. Spoon the surimi salad on top. Garnish each serving with about 3 oil-cured olives and serve.

4 SERVINGS

SALMON ROLLS

A popular hors d'oeuvre, salmon rolls are easy to make. Buy whipped cream cheese, which is easier to spread, for this recipe.

Using a good vegetable peeler, such as an Oxo, cut lengthwise strips from 1 unpeeled zucchini, stopping when you reach the seeds in the center. Rotate the zucchini and repeat this procedure. Discard the seeds. Place a long strip of zucchini on the table. Top it with a small slice of smoked salmon; it should cover only the center portion and stick out a little beyond it on either side. Spread about 2 teaspoons whipped cream cheese on the salmon and add a sprinkling of salt and freshly ground black pepper. Roll up the zucchini slice, encasing the salmon and cream cheese into a tight roll. Cut down the center and arrange both halves cut side down and green side up on a serving platter. Repeat with the remaining zucchini strips. Serve the rolls on their own or with thin sesame crackers.

SALMON MOUSSE

Smoked salmon is available freshly cut at the supermarket deli counter or prepackaged from Scotland, Alaska, Canada, or Nova Scotia. Any of these are good for this recipe. I use salmon ends or other trimmings if I can find them at a lower price, because the flesh is pureed for the mousse.

In a food processor, process 1 cup (4 to 5 ounces) smoked salmon tidbits, ends, or trimmings with ½ cup ricotta or farmer cheese, 1 teaspoon fresh lemon juice, and a good dash each of salt and freshly ground black pepper for about 45 seconds, or until smooth. Transfer to a gratin dish or deep platter. Using plastic wrap, press the mousse into the dish to create a smooth layer between ½ and 1 inch deep. Scatter 2 tablespoons finely chopped red onion, 2 teaspoons drained capers, and 1 teaspoon chopped fresh chives on top. Sprinkle with about 2 teaspoons extra-virgin olive oil. Serve with breadsticks, crostini, or pretzel crackers.

MAKES 20 TO 30 APPETIZERS

CHICKEN PERSILLADE

When I'm in the supermarket and hear an announcement that there are chickens fresh out of the rotisserie, I buy one. Plump, brown, shiny, juicy, and eminently appetizing, these chickens are good cut into pieces and served on romaine or Boston lettuce with my personal enhancement, a *persillade,* on top.

Separate the leaves of packaged, prewashed organic romaine or Boston lettuce. Spread them out on a large platter. Sprinkle with about 2 tablespoons olive oil, 2 teaspoons fresh lemon juice, salt, and freshly ground black pepper. Using kitchen shears, cut the rotisserie chicken into pieces, bones and all, and arrange on the salad. Heat 2 tablespoons olive oil and 1 tablespoon butter in a skillet. When hot, add 2 tablespoons chopped shallots and 1 tablespoon chopped garlic. Cook for about 10 seconds. Add about 3 tablespoons coarsely chopped fresh parsley, cook for 20 to 30 seconds longer, and stir in the juice from the chicken container. Spoon over the chicken pieces. Serve.

4 TO 6 MAIN-COURSE SERVINGS

GLAZED SAUSAGE BITS

This is a fast and luscious hors d'oeuvre to serve with drinks, especially strong ones like martinis, margaritas, or rum punch. Any sausage can be used, but I like the large, juicy kielbasa that I find at my local supermarket. For the glaze, I use pomegranate juice and a bit of ketchup, but you can also use orange, apple, or cranberry juice and a dash of maple syrup or honey, as well as Tabasco hot pepper sauce or cayenne pepper.

Combine ½ cup pomegranate juice, 1 tablespoon ketchup, and a good dash of Tabasco hot pepper sauce in a medium skillet. Bring to a boil and boil the mixture for 2 to 3 minutes, or until it gets syrupy. Remove the skin from a 6-ounce piece of kielbasa and cut into ½-inch-thick slices. Add the sausage slices to the sauce. Cook over high heat, turning the slices occasionally, until the mixture reduces almost completely and coats the sausage slices (2 to 3 minutes). Serve as is with toothpicks or on top of Ritz crackers.

4 SERVINGS (18 SLICES)

RICE PAPER ROLLS WITH
AVOCADO AND SUN-DRIED TOMATO

Rice papers, or spring roll wrappers, are transparent brittle disks made of rice flour. They're available at Asian markets, specialty stores, and some supermarkets. They need only 45 seconds to a minute to rehydrate in water, making them soft, pliable, and usable for quick hors d'oeuvres. They can be stuffed with shrimp, fish, meat, and vegetables, as well as cheese, ham, olives, or nuts; use whatever you have on hand. The photo is on page xiv.

Wet 16 dried rice papers under cold tap water. Set them aside for a minute to soften. Peel and pit 1 avocado and cut it into 16 wedges. Drain and set aside 16 oil-packed sun-dried tomato halves. Peel 4 scallions and cut them into 3-inch pieces. Lay the rice papers flat on the table and top each with a wedge of avocado, a sun-dried tomato half, 1 sprig fresh cilantro, and a few pieces of scallion. Sprinkle a little salt and a dash of Tabasco hot pepper sauce on each. Fold the vegetables inside the soft rice papers, bringing the sides in to make a tight, compact roll. Serve.

4 SERVINGS

CHEESY BREADSTICKS

An ideal vehicle for slightly stale bread, these "sticks" lend originality to your breadbasket and are excellent with most foods, from soup to meat to cheese.

Preheat the oven to 400 degrees. Spread about 2 tablespoons good olive oil evenly on a cookie sheet. Cut ½-inch slices from a 6-ounce piece of country-style bread. Cut each slice lengthwise into breadsticks about 1 inch wide. You should have about 2 dozen. Arrange the sticks in one layer on the oiled pan and press on them lightly. Turn the sticks over on the pan and press on them lightly again so they are oiled on both sides. In a small bowl, mix together 2 tablespoons grated Parmesan cheese and ½ teaspoon each paprika and ground cumin. Sprinkle over the breadsticks. Bake for 12 to 14 minutes, or until they are nicely browned and crisp.

MAKES ABOUT 24 BREADSTICKS

MELBA TOAST

I like my toast very thin and crunchy. If you put a very thin slice of bread in the toaster, however, it tends to burn and curl up. The solution is to use the technique Escoffier used when he created the ultrathin toast that he named Melba toast in tribute to the Australian opera singer Nellie Melba.

Cut crunchy white bread into ½-inch slices and toast. You can toast the bread twice to get it really crunchy on the outside. When the bread is toasted, trim off the crust from around it. With the bread slices arranged flat on the table, use a sharp knife held with the blade parallel to the table to cut through the soft center of each slice, giving you 2 wafer-thin slices with one toasted side and one slightly softer side. Top the soft side with butter or another spread.

CHERRIES IN EAU DE VIE

During the summer, when cherries are plump, ripe, and juicy, I put up a few jars of cherries in alcohol and keep them in the cellar to enjoy during the winter. My mother always had some preserved sour cherries or Montmorency cherries on hand. Served with some of the cherries, this eau de vie makes a great after-dinner drink. I sometimes use pure grain or fruit alcohol (about 190-proof) that I dilute by half with distilled water, but if this is not an option for you, substitute vodka instead.

Trim the stems of about 1 pound large sweet cherries such as Bing, leaving about ½ inch of stem attached to the cherries. (If the stems are pulled out, the alcohol will permeate the cherries, making them soft and mushy instead of firm and crunchy.) In a bowl, mix about ½ cup light corn syrup and 1½ cups eau de vie or vodka. Pack the cherries into a Mason jar and pour the alcohol mixture over them, adding enough so it just covers the fruit. Cover the jar with a tight-fitting lid and set aside in a cool place, such as a cellar, for at least a month. Serve a few cherries in a brandy glass with some of the liquid. The cherries will keep for a couple of years.

ABOUT 12 SERVINGS

SOUPS

BOLD AND SPICY GAZPACHO

Gazpacho is always welcome in summer. Although a garnish is not absolutely essential, I like to set aside some green pepper, onion, cucumber, and tomato along with toasted croutons to make the soup more festive. If you're pressed for time, though, process all of the vegetables and serve the soup without the garnishes. Bloody Mary mix gives the gazpacho a kick and adds complexity. The photo is on page 25.

4 SERVINGS (ABOUT 8 CUPS)

1 green bell pepper (about ½ pound)

1 Vidalia onion (about ½ pound)

3 cucumbers (about 2 pounds)

4 large ripe tomatoes (about 2 pounds)

2 garlic cloves, crushed

1½ cups Mr. & Mrs. T Bold & Spicy Bloody Mary Mix or another spicy Bloody Mary mix

1½ teaspoons salt

4 sprigs fresh fennel, dill, or parsley, for garnish

Croutons

4 ounces day-old baguette, cut into ¾-inch dice (about 1¼ cups)

1 tablespoon good olive oil

¼ teaspoon herbes de Provence

Using a vegetable peeler, remove as much of the skin as possible from the green pepper. Discard the seeds and cut the pepper into pieces. Cut enough of the pepper flesh into ½-inch dice to measure ½ cup and set aside in a small dish for the garnish. Put the remaining pepper pieces in a large blender.

Chop the onion, reserving ½ cup for the garnish. Transfer the ½ cup chopped onion to a sieve and rinse well under cold water. Drain thoroughly and set aside in a small bowl. Put the remaining onion in the blender.

Peel the cucumbers and halve them lengthwise. Using a teaspoon, scrape out the seeds and discard them. Cut enough of the cucumber flesh into ½-inch dice to measure ½ cup and set aside in a small bowl for the garnish. Cut the rest of the cucumber pieces coarsely and put them in the blender.

Cut enough tomato into 1-inch dice to measure 1¼ cups and set aside in a small bowl for the garnish. Cut the rest of the tomatoes coarsely, seeds and all, and add them to the blender. Add the garlic, Bloody Mary mix, and salt and blend until very smooth and emulsified. Push the gazpacho through a food mill if you like. You should have about 8 cups. Refrigerate until serving time.

For the croutons: Preheat the oven to 375 degrees. Scatter the bread cubes on a baking tray lined with aluminum foil. Sprinkle the bread with the oil and herbs and toss to coat the cubes. Spread the bread out evenly on the tray and bake for 10 to 12 minutes, or until nicely browned.

At serving time, stir the gazpacho well and divide it among four soup bowls. Spoon on some of the reserved diced green pepper, onion, cucumber, and tomato garnishes. Sprinkle with some croutons and top each serving with a sprig of fennel, dill, or parsley.

HEARTY VEGETABLE BEAN SOUP

As soon as the outside temperature dips below 50 degrees, I can't wait to make this vegetarian soup, which is ready in about half an hour. What goes into it is usually determined by the contents of my refrigerator: onions, leeks, scallions, carrots, celery, and salad greens are all good. Canned beans make it sturdy enough for a main course.

For a comforting lunch or dinner, serve with grated Gruyère on top and chunks of country bread as an accompaniment.

4 SERVINGS (ABOUT 6 CUPS)

4 cups water

1 medium leek, split, washed, trimmed (retaining most of the green), and cut into ½-inch pieces (about 2½ cups)

1 cup peeled and diced (½-inch) carrot

1 cup peeled and diced (½-inch) white turnip

1 cup diced (½-inch) celery

2 tablespoons good olive oil

1½ teaspoons salt

1 can (15.5 ounces) cannellini beans

1 cup grated Gruyère cheese, preferably an aged variety

Pieces of baguette or sturdy country bread

4 sprigs fresh parsley, for garnish (optional)

Combine the water, leek, carrot, turnip, celery, oil, and salt in a large saucepan or pot. Bring to a boil, cover, reduce the heat to low, and boil gently for about 12 minutes. Add the beans, including the liquid, and bring to a boil again. Boil for a few minutes. Serve in bowls with a generous sprinkling of grated Gruyère and a parsley sprig (if desired) on top and bread alongside.

SWEET POTATO SOUP

I love sweet potatoes, especially the darker variety with the rusty-colored skin and deep orange flesh. I cook them in gratins as well as in soups and I also enjoy them sliced and sautéed with honey and butter to accompany the Thanksgiving turkey. This soup can be made ahead and refrigerated or frozen. For a richer soup, substitute half-and-half for the milk, adding it just before serving.

4 SERVINGS (ABOUT 5 CUPS)

1 tablespoon safflower or olive oil

1 medium onion (6 ounces), cut into 1-inch pieces (1½ cups)

2 garlic cloves, peeled

2–3 sweet potatoes (about 2¼ pounds total), peeled and cut into 1-inch chunks

1 apple (6 ounces), peeled, cored, and coarsely sliced

1½ cups chicken stock, homemade (page 37), or low-salt canned chicken broth

2 cups water

1 cup milk

¾ teaspoon salt

¼ teaspoon Tabasco hot pepper sauce

2 tablespoons roasted sliced almonds, for garnish

4 sprigs dill or chervil, for garnish (optional)

Heat the oil in a large saucepan. Add the onion and garlic and cook over high heat for 2 minutes.

Stir in the sweet potatoes, apple, chicken stock, and water. Bring the mixture to a boil over high heat, reduce the heat to low, cover, and cook for 30 minutes, or until the sweet potato pieces are tender. Emulsify with an immersion blender until smooth. You can use a regular blender or a food processor, but an immersion blender is more convenient. (The soup can be prepared to this point a day ahead, covered, and refrigerated. It also freezes well.)

At serving time, mix in the milk, salt, and Tabasco. Heat to a boil. Divide the soup among four bowls, sprinkle each with some almonds, top with a sprig of dill, if using, and serve.

SEAFOOD CHOWDER

Good seafood chowder can be prepared in minutes. In this recipe, I use shrimp, fish, and clam juice and finish the soup with a sprinkling of crabmeat. Oysters, scallops, and mussels are good alternate choices.

The most important thing is to have a good base, of which leeks are an essential component. Mushrooms lend complexity, zucchini adds more texture, and potato flakes give a velvety smoothness and the proper thickness. The chowder can be made ahead up to the point where the fish and shellfish are added, which should be done at serving time. Bring the chowder barely back to a boil and serve immediately, with crabmeat sprinkled on as a special garnish.

4 SERVINGS (ABOUT 6 CUPS)

2 tablespoons good olive oil

1½ cups trimmed, split, washed, and sliced leeks

1 tablespoon coarsely chopped garlic

2½ cups bottled clam juice

1½ cups water

1 cup coarsely chopped white mushrooms

¾ teaspoon salt

1½ cups diced (½-inch) zucchini

1 cup instant mashed potato flakes

¾ cup 1-inch pieces peeled uncooked shrimp

1 cup 1-inch pieces boneless fish fillet

⅔ cup half-and-half

About ½ cup crabmeat, for garnish (optional)

Heat the oil in a large saucepan over high heat. When hot, add the leek and garlic and sauté for about 1 minute. Add the clam juice, water, mushrooms, and salt, bring to a boil, and boil for about 2 minutes. Stir in the zucchini and sprinkle the potato flakes on top, mixing them in with a whisk to prevent lumping. Bring to a boil and boil for about 1 minute. (The soup can be prepared several hours ahead to this point.)

At serving time, bring the soup back to a boil, add the shrimp, fish, and half-and-half and bring back just to a boil. The fish and shrimp will be cooked through. Divide among four plates or bowls and sprinkle about 2 tablespoons crabmeat, if using, onto the middle of each serving. Serve immediately.

BUTTERNUT SQUASH VELVET

Butternut is one of my favorite squashes. In this recipe, it is made into a velvety concoction that makes an elegant first course for any dinner and is good cold as well as hot. I garnish the dish with herbs and roasted pistachio nuts, although you can substitute slivered almonds. Buy peeled butternut squash if you find it at your market; it is well worth the extra money because it is difficult to peel.

4 SERVINGS (5 TO 6 CUPS)

1 butternut squash (about 1½ pounds), peeled, seeded, and cut into 2-inch pieces

¾ cup diced (1-inch) onion

1 cup sliced leek, including some of the lighter green inner leaves

1 tablespoon extra-virgin olive oil

½ teaspoon salt

¼ teaspoon freshly ground black pepper

1½ cups chicken stock, homemade (page 37), or low-salt canned chicken broth

1 cup water

½ cup heavy cream

Garnishes

¼ cup crushed pistachio nuts

A few sprigs fresh chervil, dill, chopped fresh tarragon, or chives

Put the squash, onion, leek, olive oil, salt, pepper, stock, and water in a large saucepan. Bring to a boil, cover partially, reduce the heat to low, and boil gently for 20 minutes. Emulsify with an immersion blender until smooth. You can use a regular blender or a food processor, but an immersion blender is more convenient. (The soup can be prepared to this point a day ahead, covered, and refrigerated. It also freezes well.)

At serving time, add the cream and bring the soup to a boil. Serve garnished with a sprinkling of crushed pistachios and a sprig of fresh chervil or dill or a sprinkling of tarragon or chives.

CREAM OF LEEK AND MUSHROOM SOUP

Soups are foremost dishes in my life, especially in winter. My wife and I always keep enough vegetables in our refrigerator to make a soup. Leeks are essential and our most basic soup is leek and potato in one variation or another, similar to the one that my mother and aunt used to make. In this recipe, leeks are cooked in a little oil to soften for a few minutes and the soup is finished with stock and instant mashed potato flakes.

I have a lot of chervil in my garden and, since I love the taste of it, I use it in my cooking with abandon. If you don't have access to chervil, substitute fresh parsley, basil, or chives.

4 SERVINGS (ABOUT 6 CUPS)

2 medium leeks

6 white mushrooms

2 tablespoons peanut oil

2 cups chicken stock, homemade (page 37), or low-salt canned chicken broth

2 cups water

½ teaspoon salt

½ teaspoon freshly ground black pepper

1 cup instant mashed potato flakes

1½ cups whole milk, plus more if needed

Sprigs fresh chervil, for garnish

Remove and discard most of the green outside leaves from the leeks, reserving the light green leaves from the center. Cut the leeks lengthwise into fourths and wash the leaves thoroughly under cool water to remove any dirt or sand. Slice thinly. You should have about 2 cups.

Wash the mushrooms. Slice them, stack the slices, and either cut them into thin strips or chop them coarsely.

Heat the oil in a large saucepan over high heat. Add the leeks and mushrooms and cook, or "sweat," the vegetables for 3 to 4 minutes. Add the chicken stock, water, salt, and pepper. Bring to a boil and boil for 2 to 3 minutes. Sprinkle the potato flakes on top and mix them in with a whisk to prevent lumping. Bring to a boil. (The soup can be made to this point a few hours ahead. It will thicken a lot as it sits.)

At serving time, add the milk and return to a boil. If the soup is still too thick, stir in enough additional milk to thin it to your liking. Garnish with chervil sprigs and serve.

BASIC CHICKEN STOCK

When I have a little free time on the weekend, I make this low-salt stock, defat it, and then freeze it in 2-cup batches in plastic zipper-lock bags. The stock takes a little time to simmer, but the result is well worth the time and effort. You can use uncooked chicken or turkey bones or, if you have roasted a bird, make the stock with the roasted bones. I add a bit of dark soy sauce to give a golden color to the stock.

2½ QUARTS (10 CUPS)

3 pounds chicken or turkey bones and parts (necks and backs, skinless or with as little skin as possible, and gizzards)

6 quarts lukewarm water

1 tablespoon dark soy sauce

1 large onion (about ½ pound), peeled and quartered

4 bay leaves

1 teaspoon dried thyme leaves

1 teaspoon celery seed

About ½ teaspoon whole cloves

Bring the chicken or turkey bones, parts, and water to a boil in a large stockpot over high heat. Reduce the heat to low and boil gently for 30 minutes. Most of the fat and impurities will rise to the surface during this time; skim off and discard as much as you can.

Add the remaining ingredients, return the liquid to a boil, then boil very gently over low heat, partially covered, for 2 hours. Strain the liquid through a fine-mesh sieve or through a colander lined with a dampened kitchen towel or dampened paper towels.

Allow the stock to cool. Remove the surface fat and freeze the stock in plastic zipper-lock bags. Use as needed.

ABOUT CHICKEN STOCK

If you don't have time to make homemade stock, feel free to substitute low-salt canned chicken broth for chicken stock in the recipes in this book. If you do so, however, remember that all canned broth contains some salt, so adjust the recipes accordingly.

Eggs

Cocotte Eggs with Creamed Mushrooms (opposite)　40

Mini Savory Cheesecakes on Arugula or Butterhead Lettuce　42

Gnocchi with Eggs and Scallions　44

COCOTTE EGGS WITH
CREAMED MUSHROOMS

Oeuf cocotte is an egg cooked over other ingredients in a small soufflé mold. Small Pyrex bowls or even short rocks glasses work well, too. I like to use small *pots de crème* ramekins for this recipe because the eggs look particularly beautiful prepared in them.

I put mushrooms and cheese under the eggs, but the garnishes can be varied ad infinitum: creamed chicken, shrimp, scallops, fish, or vegetable purees are among the possibilities. Aged Gruyère has a greater depth of taste than regular Swiss cheese, and it gives a special quality to this elegant first course for a dinner or main-course lunch or brunch dish. I like to serve it with the buttered sticks of bread that we call *mouillettes* in France. The photo is on page 38.

4 SERVINGS

2 tablespoons chopped shallot

1 tablespoon good olive oil

1¼ cups julienned white mushrooms

½ teaspoon salt
  Freshly ground black pepper

1 tablespoon cognac

½ cup heavy cream

3 tablespoons grated aged Gruyère, Comté, or Beaufort cheese

4 large eggs, preferably organic

2 large slices (½ inch thick) country bread, toasted well, buttered, and cut into finger-size sticks

Heat the shallot and olive oil in a small saucepan over high heat. When the mixture begins to sizzle, cook for about 30 seconds. Add the mushrooms, salt, and ¼ teaspoon pepper and cook, stirring occasionally, for about 2 minutes. Add the cognac, mix well, then add the cream and bring to a boil. Boil over high heat for 1½ to 2 minutes to reduce.

Divide the mixture in the saucepan among four small (½-cup) *pots de crème* ramekins or other small molds and sprinkle the cheese on top. (The recipe can be prepared ahead to this point.)

Just before serving time, break an egg into each ramekin and arrange the ramekins (without their lids) in a saucepan that is deep enough so the pan lid fits on top to cover the ramekins while they are cooking. Pour enough water around the ramekins in the pan to extend about ½ inch up the sides. Bring to a boil, cover the pan (not the individual ramekins), and cook for 5 to 7 minutes, or until the eggs are set but still a little runny.

To serve, place a ramekin on each of four plates and sprinkle a little freshly ground black pepper on top of the eggs, if you like. Arrange some sticks of bread around the ramekins and cover the molds with their lids if they have them, so diners have the pleasure of lifting the tops. Serve with a small espresso spoon on each plate.

MINI SAVORY CHEESECAKES
ON ARUGULA OR BUTTERHEAD LETTUCE

When I was vacationing a few years ago in Alsace, a region in northeastern France, I was surprised to see that many restaurants featured a savory *tarte au fromage*, a cheese tart made with farmer cheese and eggs and cooked in a pastry shell like a quiche. I decided to make these little savory cheesecakes in small soufflé molds. Instead of lining the molds with dough, I coat them with butter and bread crumbs, so the small cakes can be turned out easily. Serving the cheesecakes on a bed of salad lends an appealing freshness and crunch to the dish and cuts down a little on its richness. These make a great lunch or brunch main course and an elegant first course for dinner.

4 FIRST-COURSE SERVINGS

Mini Cheesecakes

- 2 teaspoons unsalted butter, softened
- 1 slice bread, processed in a food processor to make ½ cup bread crumbs
- 1 cup (one 8-ounce container) whipped cream cheese
- 2 large eggs
- ¼ cup sour cream
- ½ teaspoon salt
- ½ teaspoon freshly ground black pepper
- 2 tablespoons minced fresh parsley
- ¼ cup crumbled blue cheese, like Stilton or Roquefort

Salad

- 3 cups arugula or butterhead lettuce (Bibb or Boston leaves), or another tender, crunchy lettuce
- 1 tablespoon extra-virgin olive oil
- 1 teaspoon red wine vinegar
- Dash salt and freshly ground pepper

For the mini cheesecakes: Preheat the oven to 350 degrees. Generously coat four small (¾-cup) soufflé molds with the butter. Divide the bread crumbs among the molds and coat the bottoms and sides heavily with the crumbs, pressing them onto the buttered dish so they stick.

Put the cream cheese in a medium bowl and add the eggs, sour cream, salt, pepper, and 1 tablespoon of the parsley. Mix well with a whisk and divide among the soufflé molds. Sprinkle the crumbled blue cheese on top of the cream cheese mixture in the molds. Top with the remaining 1 tablespoon parsley.

Arrange the molds on a baking sheet and bake for about 20 minutes. The cheesecakes will still be slightly wet and soft in the center. Let cool for 10 minutes before unmolding.

For the salad: Meanwhile, toss the lettuce leaves with the oil, vinegar, and salt and pepper. Arrange on four plates.

Invert each cooled mini cheesecake into one of your hands to unmold it, then turn it over so it is right side up and place it in the center of one of the plates on top of the lettuce. Serve immediately.

GNOCCHI WITH EGGS AND SCALLIONS

Potato, eggs, and truffles are one of the most magical combinations in the kitchen, but even without truffles, potatoes and eggs are a superb match. Truffle oil from white truffles *(Tuber magnatum)* or black truffles *(T. melanosporum)* is widely available in specialty stores or on the Internet for a fairly reasonable price. White truffles from the Piedmont cost thousands of dollars a pound and the black ones, although less costly, are still expensive. They can be bought fresh during the winter season at specialty stores or over the Internet, where excellent frozen truffles can also be purchased. You can get potato gnocchi at the supermarket. Organic eggs from a farm are always the best choice.

4 SERVINGS

4 **large eggs**

12 **ounces potato gnocchi (about a dozen per person; gnocchi usually come in 1-pound packages)**

1 **cup water**

1½ **tablespoons olive oil**

1 **tablespoon unsalted butter**

½ **teaspoon salt**

½ **teaspoon freshly ground black pepper**

½ **cup minced scallions**

3 **tablespoons sour cream**

2 **tablespoons freshly grated Parmesan cheese**

About 1 tablespoon truffle oil (optional)

1 **small black truffle (frozen is fine) to shave over the dish (optional)**

Using a fork, beat the eggs in a small bowl and then set them aside. Spread the gnocchi in one layer in a large nonstick skillet and add the water, olive oil, butter, salt, and pepper. Bring to a boil, cover, and cook for about 3 minutes. Most of the water should have evaporated.

Add the scallions and continue cooking, uncovered, for 2 to 3 minutes longer, until the gnocchi and scallions start to sizzle and begin to brown lightly.

Add the eggs to the skillet and cook them, stirring constantly with a whisk, for 45 seconds to 1 minute at the most. They should be soft and loose. Add the sour cream to stop the cooking and mix it in well.

Divide the mixture among four heated plates and sprinkle with the Parmesan cheese and a few drops of truffle oil, if available. Using a vegetable peeler, shave the truffle, if you're using it, over the dish, and serve immediately.

SALADS

Asparagus Fans with Mustard
Sauce   49

Harlequin Salad   50

Tall Greek Tomato Salad
(opposite)   52

Frisée aux Lardons (Curly Endive with
Bacon Bits)   53

Tomato Surprise   56

ASPARAGUS FANS WITH MUSTARD SAUCE

I like firm, fat, green asparagus with tight heads, and I always peel the lower third of the stalks with a vegetable peeler to make them tender. I often offer this as a first course.

The asparagus is dressed with a sauce of mayonnaise, mustard, and vinegar and garnished with hard-cooked eggs and chives. Cook the asparagus fairly close to when you will sit down; it tastes better if it is served directly from the boiling water without being refreshed under cold water.

4 SERVINGS

2 large eggs
1¼ pounds large firm green asparagus
Salt
1 tablespoon minced fresh chives, for garnish

Mustard Sauce

½ cup mayonnaise
2 tablespoons Dijon mustard
2 tablespoons water
1 tablespoon red wine vinegar
Good dash freshly ground black pepper

Lower the eggs into enough boiling water to cover them and cook at a very gentle boil for 10 minutes. Drain off the water and shake the pan to crack the eggshells. Add ice to the pan and set aside for at least 15 minutes to cool completely. Shell the eggs and place them, one at a time, in an egg slicer, cut through them, then rotate them 45 degrees in the slicer and cut through them again to create strips. Alternatively, chop the eggs with a sharp knife. Set aside.

Peel the lower third of the asparagus spears with a vegetable peeler. Bring 3 cups salted water to a boil in a large skillet. Add the asparagus, cover partially, and bring back to a boil over high heat. Boil over high heat for 4 to 5 minutes, until the spears are tender but still firm. Using a slotted spatula, remove the asparagus from the water and put it on a platter.

For the sauce: Mix all the ingredients together in a small bowl.

At serving time, arrange the asparagus spears on a platter, positioning them so the stem ends are close together and the tips are fanned out. Coat the lower third of the asparagus spears with the sauce and sprinkle the eggs and chives over and around them. Serve.

HARLEQUIN SALAD

The red tomatoes are accented by the whites of hard-cooked eggs, creating a colorful harlequin effect. This quickly made, attractive first course also includes anchovy fillets, olives, and a mustard-mayonnaise sauce that complements all the salad ingredients.

4 SERVINGS

4 large eggs

Mustard-Mayonnaise Sauce

⅓ cup mayonnaise

1½ tablespoons Dijon mustard

2 tablespoons extra-virgin olive oil

1 teaspoon red wine vinegar

2 teaspoons water

¼ teaspoon salt

¼ teaspoon freshly ground black pepper

2 tomatoes (about ¾ pound total)

16 anchovy fillets

16 green olives, pitted

2 tablespoons chopped fresh chives, for garnish

Lower the eggs into enough boiling water to cover them and cook at a very gentle boil for 10 minutes. Drain the water and shake the pan to crack the eggshells. Add ice to the pan and set the eggs aside for 15 minutes to cool completely. Shell the eggs and return them to cold water.

For the sauce: Mix all the ingredients in a small bowl and then divide the sauce among four small plates.

Create a border of 4 anchovy fillets around each of the plates. Cut each egg into 4 wedges. Cut each tomato into quarters. Cut each tomato quarter almost in half horizontally, stopping when you reach the flesh adjoining the skin, so the halves are still connected. Spread the halves apart and insert a wedge of egg, white side up, in the opening. Arrange 2 of the egg-stuffed tomato quarters in the sauce on each plate and add 2 additional egg wedges, placing them yolk side up in the sauce. Set 4 olives on each plate, garnish with chives, and serve.

TALL GREEK TOMATO SALAD

The ingredients of this Greek salad are traditional but the preparation is unique. Tomatoes with the stems still attached are readily available in supermarkets. The photo is on page 47.

4 SERVINGS

Lemon–Olive Oil Dressing

- 5 tablespoons extra-virgin olive oil
- 2 tablespoons fresh lemon juice
- ½ teaspoon salt
- ½ teaspoon freshly ground black pepper

Tomato Salad

- 4 tomatoes (each about 6 ounces), with stems attached
- 1 cucumber, unpeeled, cut into ¼-inch-thick rounds
- 8 slices red onion, each about ⅛ inch thick and about the same diameter as the tomato
- Fleur de sel
- About 4 ounces feta cheese, cut into ¼-inch-thick slices about the same diameter as the tomato
- About 24 olives (a mixture of black oil-cured and kalamata)
- 2 tablespoons fresh oregano leaves, for garnish

For the dressing: Combine all the ingredients in a small bowl.

For the salad: Cut around the stems of the tomatoes with a paring knife and reserve the stem "caps" to place back on the tomatoes. Cut a small slice from the base of the tomatoes so they will sit flat after stuffing. Cut each tomato horizontally into 5 slices, each about ⅓ inch thick. (They should be cut and arranged so that the slices can be reassembled later.)

Place a bottom slice from each tomato in the center of each of four salad plates. Cover each slice with some of the cucumber slices and a slice of onion and sprinkle with fleur de sel and a little dressing. Place the second consecutive slice from each tomato on top of the first. Cover with some of the feta slices and spoon about ½ teaspoon of dressing over the cheese. Add the third slice of tomato and cover with cucumber slices, onion, and a little more dressing. Add the fourth tomato slice and cover with feta cheese and a dash of dressing. Finish by adding the last tomato slice, with the hole from the missing stem. Reinsert the stems for a nice presentation.

Divide the olives and any remaining cheese or cucumber among the plates, scattering them around the tomatoes. Sprinkle the tomatoes with some fleur de sel and any extra dressing, garnish with oregano leaves, and serve cool but not cold.

FRISÉE AUX LARDONS
(CURLY ENDIVE WITH BACON BITS)

This quintessential Lyonnaise salad is served in all the *bouchons*, or tiny cafés, throughout the French countryside. Some versions include pig's feet and herring fillets, but conventionally the salad features bacon, croutons, and poached eggs. I like to buy thick-cut bacon for mine. The best is about ¼ inch thick, available either packaged or sold as slab bacon in the supermarket delicatessen.

Frisée is curly endive or curly chicory with small jagged leaves. The greens are covered during the end of the growing cycle, so without the light or photosynthesis they turn white, like Belgian endive. The number and variety of garnishes for this salad, often served as a main course for lunch, can be altered at will.

4 SERVINGS

Mustard-Garlic Dressing

- 1½ teaspoons chopped garlic
- 1½ teaspoons Dijon mustard
- ½ teaspoon salt
- ½ teaspoon freshly ground black pepper
- 1½ tablespoons red wine vinegar
- ¼ cup extra-virgin olive oil

Salad and Garnishes

- 1 teaspoon red wine vinegar
- 4 large eggs
- 6 slices thick-cut (at least ⅛ inch) bacon
- A piece of country bread or baguette, cut into about 40 croutons, each about 1 inch square
- 1 large or 2 small heads frisée (about ½ pound total), trimmed of wilted leaves and cut into 2- to 3-inch pieces

For the dressing: Using a whisk, combine all the ingredients in a bowl large enough to hold the salad. (It is fine for the dressing ingredients to separate.)

For the salad and garnishes: Fill a small nonstick skillet with 1½ inches water. Add the red wine vinegar and bring to a boil. Break the eggs one at a time

into the water. This will stop the boiling. Reduce the heat to medium-low or low so the water doesn't boil. After about 30 seconds, move the eggs a little with a slotted spoon so they don't stick to the bottom, and continue cooking them to your liking, about 4 minutes. (They should still be runny inside.) Remove the cooked eggs from the pan with a slotted spoon and transfer them to a bowl of ice water. (The eggs can be prepared up to 2 hours ahead.)

Arrange as many bacon slices as fit in one layer on a ridged microwave tray, cooking half at a time, if necessary. Cover with a paper towel and microwave for 4 to 5 minutes, depending on how crisp you like your bacon. Cut into 1½-inch pieces.

Heat about 2 tablespoons of the bacon fat in a skillet over high heat. Add the croutons and cook, turning them so they brown on all sides, for 2 to 3 minutes. Set aside. Wash the salad greens, drain, and dry in a salad spinner.

At serving time, toss the greens well in the bowl with the dressing. Divide the salad among four plates. Lift the eggs from the bowl with a slotted spoon and place them in a sieve. Lower them into boiling water for about 1 minute to reheat them and then lift from the water. Arrange an egg in the center of each salad and sprinkle the bacon bits and croutons over the top. Serve immediately.

TOMATO SURPRISE

For this recipe, tomatoes are first blanched briefly and the skin removed. A slice is removed from the stem end, the insides are spooned out, and the tomato is filled with a mixture of vegetables, nuts, and some diced bread to absorb some of the juices. The tomatoes make a nice presentation placed stuffed side down on the serving plates, so they look whole and untouched.

4 SERVINGS

4 firm tomatoes (about 6 ounces each)

1¼ cups diced (¼-inch) white mushrooms

1¼ cups diced (¼-inch) zucchini

⅓ cup chopped onion

1 teaspoon chopped garlic

⅓ cup walnut pieces

½ cup diced (¼-inch) baguette

½ teaspoon salt

½ teaspoon freshly ground black pepper

2 tablespoons good olive oil

2 teaspoons red wine vinegar

Garnishes

⅓ cup diced (¼-inch) red onion

⅓ cup diced (¼-inch) kalamata olives or 16 pitted olives

2 tablespoons chopped fresh chives

Extra-virgin olive oil

Fleur de sel or coarse salt

4 sprigs fresh basil

Drop the tomatoes into boiling water for about 45 seconds. Drain and after a couple of minutes peel off the skin. (The skin can be kept and deep-fried in 325-degree oil for 1 minute for serving as a garnish on soup or salad.) Cut a ¼-inch slice from the stem end of each tomato. Cut the flesh from these slices into ¼-inch dice. Set these diced tomato pieces aside for use as a garnish.

Using a sharp spoon (such as a metal measuring spoon with a thin, sharp edge, a grapefruit spoon, or a melon baller), cut through the ribs inside the tomatoes and remove the flesh, seeds, and juice from the insides. (This mixture can be liquefied in a food processor to make a drink or, with the addition of salt and olive oil, to make a cold tomato soup.)

Preheat the oven to 400 degrees. Spread the diced mushrooms and zuc-chini on a baking sheet and place in the oven for 3 to 4 minutes to sweat and soften. Transfer the softened vegetables to a bowl and stir in the onion, garlic, walnuts, bread, salt, pepper, oil, and vinegar. Mix well.

Spoon the prepared stuffing into the hollowed-out tomatoes and refrig-erate, stuffed side up, until serving time.

At serving time, place the tomatoes stuffed side down on plates. Scatter the reserved diced tomatoes, red onion, olives, and chives around the tomatoes and sprinkle with the extra-virgin olive oil and fleur de sel. Garnish with the basil sprigs and serve.

FISH AND SHELLFISH

Scallop Pancakes on Boston Lettuce Salad

This unusual first course is always received well. It can be made with shrimp or fish as well as scallops, and the batter also can be cooked in teaspoon-size morsels, perfect for enjoying with drinks. Although these pancakes are delicious eaten right out of the skillet when the edges are crunchy and the centers soft, they are also tasty prepared ahead and reheated at serving time in a 450-degree oven for 4 to 5 minutes. The edges will be softer, but the pancakes are just as good. I serve them on a Boston lettuce salad as a first course for dinner or as a main dish for lunch.

4 FIRST-COURSE SERVINGS (ABOUT 12 PANCAKES)

Pancakes

- ¼ pound scallops, rinsed under cold water to remove any sand
- ½ cup all-purpose flour
- ¼ teaspoon baking powder
- 1⅓ cups club soda
- ¼ teaspoon salt
- ¼ teaspoon freshly ground black pepper
- 1 tablespoon minced fresh chives
- About 3 tablespoons peanut oil

Boston Lettuce Salad

- 2–3 cups torn Boston lettuce, washed and dried
- 1 tablespoon extra-virgin olive oil
- 1½ teaspoons fresh lemon juice
- Dash each salt and freshly ground black pepper

For the pancakes: Put the scallops, flour, baking powder, club soda, salt, and pepper in a blender or food processor and process until smooth. Stir in the chives.

Heat about 1½ tablespoons of the peanut oil in a large nonstick skillet over medium–high heat. Spoon about 1½ tablespoons batter per pancake into the pan. It will spread to form a disk about 3½ inches in diameter. Cook about 6 pancakes at a time over medium heat for a total of about 5 minutes, turning them after about 2½ minutes. Repeat with the remaining 1½ tablespoons oil and the remaining batter to make about 12 pancakes total. Transfer to a wire rack to cool for a few minutes before serving.

For the salad: Toss the lettuce with the olive oil, lemon juice, and salt and pepper in a medium bowl. To serve, divide the salad among four plates, arrange 3 pancakes alongside or on top of the greens, and serve.

BAKED CLAMS MADISON

In usual recipes for clams casino, the clams are shucked, seasoned with melted butter, scallions, and lemon juice, returned to their shells, broiled for a few minutes, and finally topped with crumbled bacon. Most of the time, clams prepared this way are tough and chewy.

In my version, named for the seacoast town where I live, the clams are tender and juicy, because they are merely warmed through. To make shucking easier, I put them in the freezer for about 15 minutes so they open readily. After being warmed in a low-temperature oven at the last minute, the clams are served with a delicious do-ahead topping.

Littlenecks or other clams that measure about 2 inches across are my favorites for this dish. The manila and mahogany varieties are usually less expensive and can be used as well.

4 FIRST-COURSE SERVINGS

2 slices bacon (2 ounces), cut into ¼-inch pieces

⅓ cup peeled and diced (¼-inch) celery

⅓ cup chopped onion

⅓ cup minced scallions

1 tablespoon chopped garlic

About ⅔ cup coarsely chopped white mushrooms

1½ tablespoons extra-virgin olive oil

⅛ teaspoon salt

¼ teaspoon freshly ground black pepper

3 tablespoons dry white wine

24 littleneck clams, or another variety measuring about 2 inches across

Sauté the bacon in a medium skillet over high heat for about 2 minutes, or until it starts to sizzle and brown. Add the celery, onion, scallions, garlic, mushrooms, olive oil, salt, and pepper and cook for about 3 minutes. Add the wine and cook for about 10 seconds longer. Set aside until serving time.

Preheat the oven to 180 degrees. Put the clams in the freezer for about 15 minutes to make shucking them easier. To shuck, run a sharp paring knife between the shells to open them and cut the adductor muscle connecting the shells. Place the meat in one of the shells and discard the other. Repeat with the remaining clams and arrange them on a baking sheet. At serving time, heat the clams in the oven for 10 to 12 minutes, or until they are lukewarm. Meanwhile, reheat the topping until it is hot. Spoon over the warm clams and serve immediately.

PICANTE MUSSEL PILAF

In this classic, the mussel meat is hidden inside small bowls of rice, which are unmolded onto individual plates, with the juice spooned around them. (You can also serve the mussels over a bed of rice.) Bloody Mary mix gives the dish spiciness and complexity.

4 SERVINGS

Mussels

> 3 **pounds mussels**
>
> 1½ **cups Bloody Mary mix**
>
> ½ **cup chopped onion**
>
> 1 **teaspoon Tabasco hot pepper sauce**
>
> ¼ **cup good olive oil**
>
> **Salt to taste**

Pilaf

> 2 **tablespoons plus 1 teaspoon good olive oil**
>
> ¼ **cup chopped onion**
>
> 1 **cup long-grain white rice**
>
> 2 **cups water**
>
> ½ **teaspoon salt**
>
> 2 **tablespoons chopped fresh parsley, for garnish**

For the mussels: Wash the mussels in a sink or large pot filled with cold water, rubbing them against each other to clean any encrustations from the shells, and remove and discard any beards. Lift the mussels from the water and put them in a large saucepan, preferably stainless steel, with the remaining ingredients.

Cook, covered, over high heat, stirring occasionally, until all the mussels have opened, about 8 minutes. Drain the mussels, reserving the broth, and remove them from the shells. (Reserve 8 of the shells for decoration, if you like.) You should have about 1½ cups mussel meat and about 1½ cups broth. Taste and add salt, if necessary. Set aside.

For the pilaf: Heat 2 tablespoons of the olive oil in a medium saucepan over high heat. Add the onion and cook for 1 minute. Stir in the rice and add the water and salt. Bring to a boil, cover, reduce the heat to low, and cook for 20 minutes. Meanwhile, oil four small ramekins or Pyrex bowls, each with about a 1-cup capacity, with the remaining 1 teaspoon of oil.

At serving time, reheat the mussels in the mussel broth. Spoon about ½ cup rice into each of the oiled bowls and spread it onto the bottom and around the sides of each bowl to create a nest in the center. Press one quarter of the mussel meat into the center

of the rice in each bowl. Press more rice on top of the mussels to enclose them, pressing well on the rice so the mixture holds together.
Unmold the rice onto four warm plates and spoon the hot mussel broth
around the rice. Sprinkle the parsley on top, decorate each plate with
mussel shells, if you like, and serve.

BAY SCALLOPS IN
MIGNONNETTE SAUCE

Try to get bay scallops for this dish, but if they are unavailable you can substitute sea scallops, cut into 4 to 6 pieces. My market usually has small Nantucket bay scallops, each about the size of a large cherry. They are very sweet, tender, and delicious raw. I marinate them for a couple of hours in a mignonnette sauce, traditionally made of shallots, coarse black pepper, and vinegar, to which I add mustard and olive oil. Pieces of crunchy, spicy radish add texture and taste. I serve this dish as a refreshing appetizer in scallop or oyster shells with a fine julienne of cucumber on top.

4 FIRST-COURSE SERVINGS

½ **pound bay scallops (about 20), rinsed under cold water to remove any sand**

2 **teaspoons red wine vinegar**

1 **teaspoon Dijon mustard**

3 **tablespoons extra-virgin olive oil**

3 **tablespoons chopped shallots**

¾ **teaspoon salt**

¾ **teaspoon coarsely ground black pepper**

1 **small cucumber**

⅓ **cup diced (¼-inch) radishes**

Remove any adductor muscles still attached to the scallops.

Combine the vinegar, mustard, oil, shallot, salt, and pepper in a bowl large enough to hold the scallops. One to 2 hours before serving time, combine the scallops with the sauce ingredients in the bowl and refrigerate.

Peel the cucumber and cut 6 to 8 long strips of flesh from it with a vegetable peeler. Pile the strips together and cut them into a fine julienne or thin, spaghetti-like strips.

At serving time, add the radish to the scallops and mix well. Divide the scallops among four scallop shells, oyster shells, or small plates and sprinkle the julienned cucumber on top. Serve.

SHRIMP WITH CABBAGE AND RED CAVIAR

When I worked as a consultant at the Russian Tea Room in New York City, I developed this dish that includes many of the ingredients used in Russian cuisine. It takes only about 10 minutes to cook. The crunchy cabbage is a perfect match for the slightly acidic sauce and both complement the shrimp.

Red salmon or trout caviar is available in some supermarkets and in specialty stores.

4 FIRST-COURSE SERVINGS

6 cups shredded savoy cabbage

1 cup chicken stock, homemade (page 37), or low-salt canned chicken broth

2 garlic cloves

¾ teaspoon salt

½ teaspoon freshly ground black pepper

¼ cup dry fruity white wine (such as Sauvignon Blanc)

¾ cup heavy cream

16 shelled uncooked jumbo shrimp (16–20 count)

1 tablespoon Dijon mustard

2 tablespoons red salmon or trout caviar

2 tablespoons chopped fresh dill, for garnish

Put the shredded cabbage in a large skillet and pour in the chicken stock. Using a Microplane or rasp grater, grate the garlic cloves over the cabbage, then add the salt and pepper and bring to a boil. Cover and boil over high heat for about 5 minutes, or until most of the liquid is gone. The cabbage should be tender but still firm.

Add the wine and cream to the skillet and boil again for about 1 minute. Add the shrimp, cover, bring back to a boil, and cook for 1 to 2 minutes. The shrimp should be pink and firm. Add the mustard and stir it into the sauce to thicken it.

Spoon the cabbage onto four warm plates and arrange the shrimp and sauce over it. Garnish each serving with about ½ tablespoon caviar and a sprinkling of dill and serve.

BLUEFIN TUNA TARTARE
WITH APPLE

Especially for dishes like tartare, ceviche, and gravlax, the fresher the fish, the better the result. For this recipe, I start with a tuna steak about 1 inch thick and cut it into ½-inch squares. Using larger pieces rather than finely chopped fish, the conventional choice, gives the dish a creamier feel in the mouth. Do not mix the ingredients together more than 1 to 2 hours before serving; if combined sooner, the lemon juice will discolor the tuna, turning it an opaque white.

4 FIRST-COURSE SERVINGS

¾ pound tuna steak, preferably bluefin or yellowtail, about 1 inch thick

1 small apple, such as Granny Smith

¼ cup finely chopped shallots

½ teaspoon finely chopped garlic

¾ teaspoon salt

½ teaspoon freshly ground black pepper

¼ teaspoon Tabasco hot pepper sauce

1 teaspoon lemon zest

1½ teaspoons fresh lemon juice

2½ tablespoons extra-virgin olive oil

2 tablespoons finely chopped fresh chives

1 small cucumber

Cut the tuna steak into ¼-inch-thick slices, then cut each slice into ½-inch squares. Peel the apple and cut the flesh into ¼-inch pieces. You should have about ⅔ cup.

No more than 2 hours before serving, mix together in a medium bowl the tuna, apple, shallots, garlic, salt, pepper, Tabasco, lemon zest, lemon juice, olive oil, and chives.

Peel the cucumber with a vegetable peeler. Use the peeler to cut 9 long strips of flesh from the cucumber, pivoting the cucumber and stopping before you reach the seeds in the center. Julienne 1 cucumber strip and set aside for the garnish. Mound the tuna tartare in the center of each of four plates and wrap 2 cucumber strips around each mound to enclose it. Garnish with some of the julienned cucumber and serve.

LOBSTER ROLL MEDALLIONS
ON SPINACH SALAD

One of the treats of my summers in Connecticut is the lobster rolls that I enjoy at the Clam Castle, a small shoreline restaurant in Madison, where I live. The lobster is piled into New England–style hot dog rolls and the flat sides of the filled rolls are browned gently in butter. My fishmonger has fresh, tender, cooked lobster meat available most of the year, but this recipe also can be made with cooked shrimp. The lobster rolls are cooked whole and then cut into thick medallions and served on a bed of baby spinach. For a fancier version, the hot dog rolls can be replaced by brioche rolls.

4 FIRST-COURSE SERVINGS

Lobster Rolls

- 4 tablespoons (½ stick) unsalted butter
- ¼ cup chopped shallots
- ¼ cup finely chopped scallions
- ½ pound cooked lobster meat, cut into ¾-inch pieces
- ¼ teaspoon salt
- ¼ teaspoon freshly ground black pepper
- 4 New England–style hot dog rolls

Spinach Salad

- 3 cups (lightly packed) baby spinach, washed and dried
- 1 tablespoon extra-virgin olive oil
- 1 teaspoon fresh lemon juice
  Dash salt and freshly ground black pepper

For the lobster rolls: Melt 2 tablespoons of the butter in a small skillet over high heat. Add the shallots and scallions and cook for about 1 minute. Transfer to a medium bowl and mix in the lobster meat, salt, and pepper.

Divide the filling among the 4 rolls, spooning it evenly inside and then pressing the sides of the rolls together to enclose the filling.

Preheat the oven to 400 degrees. Line a baking sheet with foil. Butter the filled rolls on both sides with the remaining 2 tablespoons butter and arrange the rolls on the baking sheet. Bake for 10 minutes, or until well browned on both sides. Remove from the oven and set aside for 5 minutes to cool a little while you make the salad.

For the salad: In a medium bowl, mix the spinach with the oil, lemon juice, and salt and pepper. Divide the salad among four plates.

Trim off both ends of the lobster rolls and cut each roll crosswise into 4 pieces. Arrange 4 medallions stuffed side up on each salad and serve.

SMALL CROCKS OF SHRIMP IN HOT VEGETABLE BROTH

Although I love shrimp cocktail, shrimp that are boiled in water or steamed often lack flavor. I poach my shrimp in a spicy vegetable broth and let them cool in the broth so they become permeated with the taste of the vegetables. The broth is so tasty that I serve the shrimp in it.

Because shrimp cooked in the shell have more flavor, I prefer to use "easy-peel" shrimp, which are available in many markets. Their shells are cut along the back and the shrimp are already deveined. The shells slide off easily after cooking, so I consider this finger food.

Two horseradish sauces, one red and one white, enhance the shrimp and broth, which are served warm in small glass bowls or ceramic crocks.

4 MAIN-COURSE SERVINGS

Shrimp in Vegetable Broth

- 2 cups water
- 1/3 cup diced (1/4-inch) celery
- 1/3 cup peeled and diced (1/4-inch) carrot
- 1/3 cup diced (1/4-inch) onion
- 1/2 cup diced (1/4-inch) leek
- 1/3 cup chopped fresh parsley leaves
- 1/4 teaspoon red pepper flakes
- 1/2 teaspoon salt
- 1 tablespoon red wine vinegar
- 1 pound uncooked large shrimp (21–25 count), with shells on

Red Horseradish Sauce

- 1/3 cup ketchup
- 2 tablespoons grated fresh or bottled horseradish
- 1 teaspoon fresh lemon juice
- 1/4 teaspoon Tabasco hot pepper sauce

White Horseradish Sauce

- 1/3 cup sour cream
- 1 tablespoon grated fresh or bottled horseradish
- 1 teaspoon fresh lemon juice
- 1/4 teaspoon salt
- 1/4 teaspoon freshly ground black pepper

For the shrimp in broth: Put all the ingredients except the shrimp in a large saucepan and bring to a boil. Reduce the heat and boil gently, uncovered, for about 3 minutes. Add the shrimp, mix well, and return just to a boil. As soon as the liquid starts boiling

(it will take 1 to 2 minutes), remove the pan from the heat, cover, and let the shrimp cool in the broth.

For the horseradish sauces: Combine the ingredients for each sauce in separate small serving dishes or bowls.

At serving time, warm the shrimp in the stock until tepid and divide them and the broth among four crocks or small glass bowls. Serve with the two horseradish sauces, with spoons for the broth. Diners can eat the shrimp with their fingers.

Scallops Grenobloise

A traditional sauce for fish and shellfish, grenobloise consists of diced lemon flesh, capers, and croutons. Here I add mushrooms. This recipe is a winner and works equally well with fish or shrimp. I prefer to use large diver scallops from a reputable fishmonger. Avoid scallops with milky juice seeping out of them, an indication that they have been soaked in a solution to plump them, often the mark of inferior quality.

8 FIRST-COURSE SERVINGS OR 4 MAIN-COURSE SERVINGS

2 slices white bread

2½ tablespoons peanut or canola oil

1 lemon

1 pound large scallops (about 16), rinsed under cold water to remove any sand

½ teaspoon salt

½ teaspoon freshly ground black pepper

2 tablespoons drained capers

6 tablespoons (¾ stick) unsalted butter

¼ cup diced (½-inch) white mushrooms (about 3)

1 tablespoon red wine vinegar

2 tablespoons coarsely chopped fresh parsley, for garnish

Preheat the oven to 350 degrees. Cut the bread into ½-inch dice and toss the bread with 1 tablespoon of the oil. Spread the pieces on a cookie sheet and bake for 6 to 8 minutes, or until browned. Set aside.

Peel the lemon, removing the skin and the white pith underneath. Cut between the membranes to remove totally clean segments of lemon flesh. Cut into ½-inch pieces until you have about 2 tablespoons diced lemon flesh.

Remove any adductor muscles still attached to the scallops. Sprinkle them with the salt, pepper, and the remaining 1½ tablespoons oil. Heat a large nonstick skillet over high heat until very hot, then add the scallops. Reduce the heat to medium and cook for about 2 minutes on each side. They should be nicely browned. Arrange 4 scallops on each of four serving plates and sprinkle on the lemon pieces, capers, and bread cubes.

Heat the butter in a small skillet and add the mushrooms. Cook for 2 to 4 minutes, or until the butter browns lightly (this is called noisette butter). Add the vinegar. Spoon the sauce over the scallops, sprinkle the parsley on top, and serve.

GRILLED STRIPED BASS WITH ROMESCO SAUCE

I grill thick fillets of fish such as striped bass, tautog (also known as blackfish), sea bass, or red snapper and serve them with romesco sauce, a traditional Spanish sauce made of chile peppers, almonds, tomato, garlic, and olive oil. If a grill is not available, the fillets can be broiled instead. The sauce is great with any poached or grilled fish or meat. In my version, I use ancho peppers; flavorful and mildly hot, they are the dried form of fresh poblano peppers. This sauce freezes well.

4 SERVINGS

Romesco Sauce

- 1 small ancho chile pepper
- ¼ cup good olive oil
- ½ cup diced onion
- 3 tablespoons whole almonds
- 2 teaspoons sliced garlic
- 1 jalapeño chile pepper, halved, seeds removed if desired
- 1 cup diced (1-inch) tomato
- ½ teaspoon salt
- 1 tablespoon red wine vinegar
- ¼ cup water

Grilled Fish

- 4 fish fillets (each about 6 ounces and ¾-inch thick) from striped bass, blackfish, sea bass, or red snapper
- ¾ teaspoon salt
- 1½ tablespoons olive oil
- 1 tablespoon minced fresh chives, for garnish

For the romesco sauce: Wash the ancho chile, cut it open, and remove and discard the seeds and stem. Break the ancho chile into 1-inch pieces; you should have about ¼ loosely packed cup.

Heat the oil in a small skillet over high heat. Add the onion, almonds, ancho pieces, garlic, and jalapeño. Cook for about 2 minutes, then add the tomato and salt and cook for another 2 to 3 minutes. Add the vinegar and water and boil for about 1 minute longer. Transfer to a blender and emulsify into a smooth puree. You will have about 1 cup.

For the grilled fish: Preheat a grill and preheat the oven to 170 degrees. Pat the fillets dry with paper towels, sprinkle them with salt, and rub them with the olive oil. Arrange the fillets on the rack of a very hot, very clean grill. Cook for about 2 minutes, then turn and cook for 2 minutes on the other side, or until still slightly uncooked in the center. Transfer to a baking sheet and keep warm in the oven. At serving time, arrange a fillet on each of four plates, sprinkle with the chives, and serve with a few generous spoonfuls of romesco sauce.

STEAMED SCROD PACKAGES IN PIMIENTO SAUCE

My wife, Gloria, often uses rice papers to make her Vietnamese and Chinese specialties. In this recipe, I wrap them around scrod, cod, or haddock, which can be used interchangeably. The dish is also good made with other fish, from bass to salmon. The fish packages can be assembled a few hours ahead and steamed at serving time.

The red sauce is prepared in seconds. Dried rice papers, also called spring roll wrappers, are found in specialty stores and some supermarkets as well.

4 SERVINGS

A few lettuce leaves to line the steamer

4 rice papers (about 8½ inches in diameter)

½ teaspoon salt

½ teaspoon freshly ground black pepper

4 pieces (5–6 ounces each and about 1 inch thick) scrod, haddock, or cod

4 fresh basil leaves

Pimiento Sauce

1 red pimiento, cut into ½-inch dice (about ½ cup)

¼ cup water

¼ teaspoon salt

¼ teaspoon freshly ground black pepper

2 tablespoons extra-virgin olive oil

1 tablespoon unsalted butter, at room temperature

Line a steamer basket with the lettuce leaves to help prevent the fish packages from sticking. Set the steamer basket over a pan of water and bring the water to a boil.

Wet the rice papers with water and place them side by side on the table. They will soften in a minute or so. Meanwhile, salt and pepper the fish. Place 1 basil leaf in the center of each of the rice papers and put a piece of fish on top. Wrap the fish in the rice paper and place the packages seam side down in the steamer basket. Cover and steam for 4 to 5 minutes. They will be barely cooked inside.

For the pimiento sauce: Put the pimiento, water, salt, pepper, and oil in a medium glass bowl and, using an immersion blender or a regular one, blend into a smooth puree. Heat in a microwave oven for 1½ to 2 minutes. Add the butter and mix it in with the blender.

Place each fish package in the center of a warm plate, pour some sauce around it, and serve immediately.

ONION-CRUSTED SOLE WITH ANCHOVY BUTTER

While dining at a friend's home, I enjoyed a pan-fried fish with a crusty coating that had great flavor and beautiful color. It turned out that the crust was made of fried onions. I thought this was a brilliant idea, and my recipe, made with canned fried onions, is based on that taste memory. Select whatever flatfish is freshest at your fish market, from lemon sole to gray sole to plaice or fluke or Dover sole (the best!). Any thin, flat, white fish fillet, from John Dory to turbot, will work well.

The anchovy butter is great served with grilled, broiled, or pan-fried fish and it is just as good with grilled meat. It will keep refrigerated for a week or so and can be frozen.

4 SERVINGS

Anchovy Butter

- 1 can (2 ounces) anchovy fillets in oil
- 1 large garlic clove, sliced
- 4 tablespoons (½ stick) unsalted butter, at room temperature
- ¼ teaspoon freshly ground black pepper
- 1 tablespoon dry white wine

Sole

- 2 large eggs
- 4 sole fillets (each about 6 ounces)
- ½ teaspoon salt
- 1 can (6 ounces) french-fried onions
- 3 tablespoons canola or peanut oil
- 1 lemon, quartered

For the anchovy butter: Process all the ingredients in a food processor or mini chopper until smooth and creamy. If not serving immediately, refrigerate.

For the sole: Beat the eggs in a shallow bowl until smooth and well combined. Pat the fish fillets with paper towels to dry them thoroughly. Sprinkle both sides with the salt. Put the fried onions in a food processor and process until smooth and powdery. Transfer the onion mixture to a large plate or cookie sheet.

Heat the oil in a large nonstick skillet or divide the oil between two slightly smaller skillets. Dip the fish fillets in the eggs and then into the powdered onion. Arrange in one layer in the skillet(s) and cook for 1½ to 2 minutes on each side, until well browned and barely cooked in the center, turning carefully with a large spatula. Transfer to warm plates and serve each with a lemon wedge and a spoonful of anchovy butter on the side.

COD IN OLIVE-TOMATO CRUST

You can take liberties with the crust for this dish: I sometimes add horserad-ish, bread crumbs, minced scallions, herbs, and garlic, for example. The as-sertive ingredients in this crust are just right for flaky and mild-flavored cod. Scrod and haddock also work well. In fact, any fresh fish fillets—the fresher the better—can be cooked this way.

I like to buy cod loin fillets, which are the thick ones from the back of the fish. About 1 inch thick, they will need 5 to 6 minutes under the broiler; adjust the timing if your fillets are thinner or thicker. The dish can be assembled a few hours ahead so it is ready to slide under the broiler at serving time.

Serve with Skillet Broccoli Bits (page 124).

4 SERVINGS

About ½ cup oil-packed sun-dried tomato halves, drained

About ½ cup pitted black olives

2 tablespoons grated Parmesan cheese

4 cod loin fillets (about 6 ounces each)

1 tablespoon extra-virgin olive oil, plus more to drizzle on at the table

½ teaspoon salt

¼ teaspoon freshly ground black pepper

2 tablespoons chopped fresh parsley, for garnish

Preheat the broiler and line a baking sheet with alu-minum foil. Cut the tomatoes into 1-inch pieces and put them in a food processor with the olives and cheese. Process until you have a rough puree that holds together.

Rub the fillets with the 1 tablespoon oil and sprinkle them with the salt and pepper. Arrange the fillets so there is space between them on the baking sheet. Cover the fillets with the tomato-olive mixture and slide them under the broiler, so the fish is about 4 inches from the heat source. Broil for about 5 minutes, until the fillets are just tender but are still slightly undercooked inside. Garnish with the parsley and serve. Pass the bottle of extra-virgin olive oil at the table.

POACHED SALMON IN
SOUR CREAM–HERB SAUCE

A simple poached salmon, slightly underdone, is one of the easiest dishes to prepare and is certainly one of the most delectable. Choose the freshest fish you can find. The steaks should be about the same thickness so they cook in the same amount of time.

The simple sauce of mayonnaise and sour cream with herbs is excellent with all poached fish. Serving the salmon on a thin bed of zucchini gives the dish a bit of complexity and eye appeal.

4 SERVINGS

1 firm medium zucchini, trimmed and sliced lengthwise with a Japanese vegetable slicer or a good vegetable peeler into 16 thin slices

Salt

½ cup mayonnaise

⅓ cup sour cream

1 tablespoon finely chopped fresh chives

¼ teaspoon freshly ground black pepper

4 salmon steaks (about 5 ounces each and 1 inch thick), preferably from the thick back fillet

Preheat the oven to 350 degrees. Line a cookie sheet with aluminum foil. Arrange the zucchini slices in one layer on the cookie sheet and sprinkle them with ¼ teaspoon salt. Bake for about 3 minutes, or until the slices soften.

Mix the mayonnaise, sour cream, chives, ¼ teaspoon salt, and the pepper together in a bowl. Set aside.

At serving time, bring 4 cups salted water to a boil in a large saucepan or skillet and add the salmon steaks. Cook for about 4 minutes, uncovered. The liquid should barely boil. When probed gently with a fork, the steaks should be slightly undercooked inside. Lift fish from the water and set aside in a warm place.

Warm the zucchini slices in a microwave oven for 45 seconds. Arrange 4 slices in a grid or other interesting pattern on each of four plates and place a salmon steak in the middle. Top with a little sauce and pass extra sauce at the table.

SALMON BURGERS ON BABY ARUGULA

Salmon is widely available in supermarkets, but I tend to go to my fishmonger for better quality. Price and quality can vary widely from farm-raised to wild. As always, freshness is the most important factor.

Buy a piece of salmon that is about 20 ounces so that when you discard the skin, sinews, and any fins, it will weigh about 1 pound, enough for 4 ounces per person. The salmon, bread, mushrooms, and scallions should all be cut into pieces between ½ and 1 inch before being put in the food processor. It should take only a few seconds for the mixture to stick together.

4 SERVINGS

Salmon

- 1 pound totally clean salmon fillet, pinbones removed, cut into 1-inch chunks
- 2 slices white sandwich bread, cut into cubes (1 cup)
- 1 cup diced white mushrooms
- ½ cup chopped scallions
- ¾ teaspoon salt
- ½ teaspoon freshly ground black pepper
- 1 tablespoon good olive oil

Salad

- 4 cups baby arugula
- 1 tablespoon extra-virgin olive oil
- 2 teaspoons sherry vinegar
- ¼ teaspoon salt
- ¼ teaspoon freshly ground black pepper

For the salmon: Put all the ingredients except the olive oil in a food processor and process for a few seconds, just until the mixture starts sticking together but remains chunky. Divide the mixture into fourths and shape each into a 4-inch-diameter burger about ¾ inch thick.

At cooking time, heat the olive oil over medium heat in a large nonstick skillet and arrange the burgers in one layer in the pan. Cook, uncovered, for about 2 minutes on each side; the burgers should be slightly undercooked in the center.

For the salad: Meanwhile, toss the baby arugula in a large bowl with the olive oil, vinegar, salt, and pepper. Divide the salad among four plates. Place a burger in the center of each salad and serve.

FILLET OF SOLE WITH
MUSHROOM SAUCE

In this recipe, strips of fillet of sole are rolled to form what French cooks call *paupiettes*. Rolled beginning at the thickest end, the *paupiettes* will not unfurl as they cook. Using whipped butter makes the preparation easier, because when the butter boils it holds together without breaking down as regular butter might.

The traditional version is made with wine, cream, and mushrooms, but Sole Normande can include cider, tomatoes, herbs, or even cooked apple, all Normandy products.

Any of the different types of flatfish available, from gray to lemon to Dover sole and from fluke to flounder, are fine for this recipe; the important consideration is freshness.

4 SERVINGS

4 large sole fillets (about 5 ounces each)

2 cups sliced white mushrooms

⅓ cup sliced scallions

⅓ cup sliced shallots

½ teaspoon salt

½ teaspoon freshly ground black pepper

1 cup dry white wine

½ cup whipped unsalted butter

1 tablespoon chopped fresh chives, for garnish

Cut each fillet in half lengthwise, removing and discarding the small strip of sinew from the center of the fillets. With the white side that touched the bones on the outside of the *paupiettes,* roll up the fillets, starting at the thick end.

Gently place the *paupiettes* and the remaining ingredients, except the butter and chives, in a medium saucepan and bring to a boil over high heat. Cover, reduce the heat, and boil gently for about 3 minutes.

Holding the lid so the *paupiettes* remain in the pan, pour the cooking liquid into a small saucepan and place it over high heat. Boil for a few minutes, or until the liquid is reduced to about ⅓ cup. Add the whipped butter and mix in well with a whisk. Bring to a boil and boil for a few seconds.

Divide the *paupiettes* and mushrooms among four warm plates, pour the sauce on top, and sprinkle on the chives. Serve immediately.

STEAMED FISH
AND SHELLFISH BASKETS

My wife, Gloria, still raves about a meal she enjoyed in a starred seafood restaurant in France. It consisted of steamed shellfish and fish served in their individual bamboo steamers. The small steamers, about 7 inches in diameter, are available in most Asian markets. Alternatively, the whole fish and shellfish mixture can be steamed together in one 12-inch-diameter steamer, which can be placed in the middle of the table so guests can help themselves.

It's important to line the steamer basket so the seafood doesn't stick to the bamboo. I get seaweed from the beach near my Connecticut home, but most fish markets have it or you can line the basket with salad greens.

I use shrimp, scallops, mussels, and codfish here, but any fresh fish or shell-fish, from squid to clams, salmon, or sole, can be substituted. Choose whatever is freshest and steam it "naturally," meaning without salt, pepper, or any seasonings. I serve my baskets with butter and olive oil, both flavored with lemon juice. Choose one or try them both. I offer coarse salt, such as kosher or fleur de sel, at the table as well.

4 SERVINGS

6–8 cups seaweed (see headnote)

½ pound shelled uncooked shrimp (about 12), deveined if necessary

½ pound bay scallops (Nantucket scallops are great) or sea scallops, halved or quartered, depending on size

12 mussels, washed and debearded

¾ pound cod, cut into 4 pieces

Lemon–Olive Oil Sauce

2 teaspoons fresh lemon juice

3 tablespoons extra-virgin olive oil

¼ teaspoon salt

¼ teaspoon freshly ground black pepper

Lemon-Butter Sauce

3 tablespoons unsalted butter, melted

2 tablespoons fresh lemon juice

¼ teaspoon salt

¼ teaspoon freshly ground black pepper

Fleur de sel or kosher salt

Line four individual bamboo steamer baskets with seaweed. In each basket, place 3 shrimp, 3 or 4 small scallops, 3 mussels, and 1 piece of fish. About 10 minutes before serving time, stack the steamers and place them over boiling water in a skillet or small wok that is not larger than the steamer baskets so the emerging steam will go up through the center of the baskets rather than around them, as it would if a larger skillet were used. Steam for 7 to 8 minutes, checking occasionally to see if the fish is done; it should be quite moist and barely cooked in the center.

For the lemon–olive oil sauce: Whisk all the ingredients together in a small bowl.

For the lemon-butter sauce: Whisk all the ingredients together in a small bowl.

Place a steamer basket on each of four dinner plates and serve with the two sauces and some coarse fleur de sel or kosher salt.

SHELLFISH AND CHICKEN PAELLA

Paella is arguably the national dish of Spain, and the best ones, it is said, come from Valencia in the south. Gloria and I had our best paella there in an unassuming little restaurant where the lady owner was the chef.

I have made paella with all varieties of rice, although conventionally it is made with Spanish short-grain. Italian Arborio rice, French rice from Camargue, and Asian or American rice work as well.

Although true paella is made in a shallow tin pan on an open fire and can include rabbit as well as snails or eel, I make mine with chorizo sausage and chicken thighs, adding shellfish at the last moment. I also cover the pan, which is not the traditional procedure, because this helps the mixture cook more evenly. The chicken, chorizo, mushrooms, onion, and garlic can be browned a couple of hours ahead.

I like to use commercial *alcaparrado*, a mixture of olives, red pimientos, and capers that my wife uses in her Caribbean cooking, and hot salsa, both of which are available in markets.

4 SERVINGS

- 3 tablespoons good olive oil
- 1 chorizo sausage (about ¼ pound), skinned and cut into 12 slices
- 4 small skinless chicken thighs (about 1 pound total)
- 1 cup diced (½-inch) white mushrooms
- 1 cup coarsely chopped onion
- 1 tablespoon coarsely chopped garlic
- 1¼ cups short-grain rice (Spanish, Italian, French, Asian, or American)
- 1 cup *alcaparrado*, drained and rinsed under cold water, or a mixture of equal parts diced green olives, red pimiento, capers, and garlic

- 1 cup canned diced tomatoes in sauce
- About 1½ teaspoons saffron pistils
- ⅓ cup hot salsa
- 1¼ cups chicken stock, homemade (page 37), or low-salt canned chicken broth
- 1¼ teaspoons salt
- 20 mussels (about 14 ounces total), washed and debearded
- 5 large sea scallops (about 6 ounces total), rinsed under cold water to remove any sand
- 12 uncooked large shrimp (about ½ pound total), with shells left on
- ½ cup frozen petite peas

Heat the oil in a large saucepan. Add the chorizo and chicken and brown over high to medium heat for 5 minutes, turning to brown on all sides. Add the mushrooms, onion, and garlic, and cook for 1 minute. (The recipe can be prepared to this point a couple of hours ahead.)

About 30 minutes before serving time, reheat the mixture until it sizzles. Add the rice to the pan and mix well. Stir in the *alcaparrado,* tomatoes, saffron, hot salsa, chicken stock, and salt. Mix well and bring to a boil. Cover, reduce the heat to low, and cook for about 12 minutes.

Add the mussels, scallops, and shrimp to the pan, placing them on top of the rice without stirring them in. Cover, increase the heat to medium, and cook for an additional 8 minutes. Add the peas, cover, and cook for 3 minutes longer. Stir well and divide among four warm plates. Serve.

POULTRY AND MEAT

CHICKEN SUPRÊMES WITH TAPENADE AND MUSHROOM SAUCE

Skinless, boneless chicken breasts are called *suprêmes* in French cooking. Some markets offer organic or free-range chicken, which is my choice for this recipe. Tapenade is a Provençal mixture of olives, capers, and anchovy fillets. To mine I add a little garlic and some apricots for a bit of zing and sweetness. While tapenade is excellent served on toast or baguette slices with aperitifs, it is used here as a stuffing for chicken breasts. The breasts can be stuffed ahead and sautéed at the last moment.

I often use wild mushrooms for the sauce in summer because hunting for mushrooms in the woods is one of my greatest pleasures. Baby bellas, creminis, or regular white ones are perfectly fine, though, for this dish.

4 SERVINGS

Tapenade

- ¾ cup mixed pitted black oil-cured, kalamata, and green olives
- 1 small garlic clove, sliced
- 2 dried apricot halves, cut into small pieces
- 1½ tablespoons drained capers
- 8 anchovy fillets in oil
- 2 tablespoons extra-virgin olive oil

- 4 skinless, boneless chicken breasts (about 6 ounces each)
- 1 tablespoon good olive oil
- 4 tablespoons (½ stick) unsalted butter
  Salt and freshly ground black pepper
- 1½ cups baby bella mushrooms, washed and cut into ¾-inch pieces
- ½ cup chopped onion
- ½ cup dry white wine
- 2 tablespoons chopped fresh chives or parsley, for garnish

For the tapenade: Put all the ingredients in a food processor and pulse to make a coarse puree.

Cut a horizontal slit in each chicken breast to create a pocket and stuff with the tapenade.

When ready to cook the chicken, preheat the oven to 180 degrees. Heat the olive oil and 2 tablespoons

of the butter in a large skillet. Meanwhile, season the stuffed chicken breasts with ½ teaspoon each salt and pepper and arrange them side by side in the hot skillet. Cook over medium heat, covered, for about 3 minutes on each side. Transfer to a platter. Keep warm in the oven.

Add the mushrooms and onion to the skillet and sauté for about 2 minutes. Add the wine and reduce by boiling for 2 minutes. Add the remaining 2 tablespoons butter and salt and pepper to taste and mix well to incorporate the butter.

Serve a chicken breast on each of four hot plates. Add any juice that has accumulated around them on the platter to the mushroom sauce in the pan. Spoon the mushrooms and sauce over the chicken breasts and sprinkle the parsley on top. Serve.

CRUSTY CHICKEN THIGHS WITH MUSHROOM SAUCE

Thighs are the part of the chicken that I enjoy most. When I cook them in stews or with a sauce, I remove the skin because when it is cooked with moisture, it gets rubbery and releases all its fat into the sauce.

In this recipe, I cook the thighs in a skillet skin side down, so the skin becomes crisp, dry, and beautifully browned. Make sure to use a nonstick skillet with a tight-fitting lid, so as the skin fries, the flesh is cooked by the steam. The portions are relatively small here, but within the context of a menu this is enough meat.

4 SERVINGS

4 large chicken thighs (about 1¾ pounds total), skin on

¾ teaspoon salt

¾ teaspoon freshly ground black pepper

1 cup diced (¼-inch) onion

1½ tablespoons coarsely chopped garlic

3 cups washed and diced (½-inch) baby bella or white mushrooms

⅓ cup dry white wine

1 tablespoon chopped fresh chives, for garnish

Arrange the chicken thighs skin side down on a cutting board. Using a sharp paring knife, trim off any excess skin at the edges and cut about ½ inch deep into the flesh on either side of the thigh bone. (This will help the meat cook more quickly.) Sprinkle the thighs with ½ teaspoon each of the salt and pepper and arrange them skin side down in one layer in a nonstick skillet with a tight-fitting lid.

Place the skillet over high heat and when the thighs start sizzling reduce the heat to medium, cover tightly, and cook for 16 to 18 minutes, checking occasionally to make sure the chicken is browning properly. Meanwhile, preheat the oven to 150 degrees. If the chicken seems to be cooking too fast after 10 minutes or so, reduce the heat to low. The skin of the chicken should be very crisp and brown. Transfer the chicken skin side up to an ovenproof platter and place it in the oven.

Discard all but 2 tablespoons fat from the skillet in which you cooked the chicken. Add the onion, garlic, and mushrooms and sauté them over high

heat for about 3 minutes. Sprinkle the remaining ¼ teaspoon salt and ¼ teaspoon pepper on the mushrooms and then add the wine and any liquid that has accumulated around the thighs on the platter. Cook the sauce over high heat for about 1 minute to reduce the liquid.

To serve, divide the sauce among four hot plates. Place a thigh in the middle of the mushroom sauce on each plate, spoon some sauce over, sprinkle on the chives, and serve.

ROASTED SPLIT CHICKEN WITH MUSTARD CRUST

I often make this recipe at home when I am in a hurry, because splitting and flattening the chicken and cutting between the joints of the leg and the shoulder reduce the cooking time by half. I use kitchen shears to split the chicken open at the back and to cut the cooked bird into serving pieces and a knife to cut between the joints.

The mustard crust can be made ahead and even spread on the chicken a day ahead, if you like. I pour the cooked chicken juices into a fat separator with a spout and serve over Fluffy Mashed Potatoes, leaving the fat behind.

4 SERVINGS

Mustard Crust

- 2 tablespoons chopped garlic
- 2 tablespoons Dijon mustard
- 2 tablespoons dry white wine
- 1 tablespoon soy sauce
- 2 tablespoons olive oil
- 1 teaspoon Tabasco hot pepper sauce
- 1 teaspoon herbes de Provence
- ½ teaspoon salt

- 1 chicken (about 3½ pounds)
  Fluffy Mashed Potatoes (page 142; optional)

For the crust: Mix all the ingredients in a small bowl.

Preheat the oven to 450 degrees. Using kitchen shears or a sharp knife, cut alongside the backbone of the chicken to split it open. Spread and press on the chicken with your hands to flatten it. Using a sharp paring knife, cut halfway through both sides of the joints connecting the thighs and drumsticks and cut through the joints of the shoulder under the wings as well. (This will help the heat penetrate these joints and accelerate the cooking process.)

Put the chicken skin side down on a cutting board and spread it with about half the mustard mixture. Place the chicken flat in a large skillet, mustard side down. Spread the remaining mustard on the skin side of the chicken. Cook over high heat for about 5 minutes, then place the skillet in the oven and cook

the chicken for about 30 minutes. It should be well browned and dark on top.

Let the chicken rest in the skillet at room temperature for a few minutes, then cut it into 8 pieces with clean kitchen shears. Defat the cooking juices. If you like, mound some Fluffy Mashed Potatoes on each of four warm dinner plates and place 2 pieces of chicken on each plate. Pour some juice on the mashed potatoes and chicken and serve.

TURKEY SCALOPPINE WITH DRIED MORELS

This classic dish used to be made with veal. Nowadays, it is hard to find in supermarkets and very expensive. Turkey is an inexpensive alternative that is tender if not overcooked.

Dried morels are more flavorful than fresh and the soaking liquid used to reconstitute them adds intensity to the sauce. I usually rinse the morels briefly under running water to remove any surface dust or dirt before I put them in a bowl to soak. Take care to pour them and their soaking water into the skillets slowly, and discard the last few tablespoons of liquid, along with any sand or dirt that has settled to the bottom. You can substitute other dried mushrooms, like porcini (cèpes) or shiitakes.

4 SERVINGS

1 cup dried morels (about 1 ounce)

1½ cups tepid water

2 tablespoons unsalted butter

2 tablespoons canola oil

4 large or 8 small turkey scaloppine or cutlets (about 1 pound total)

¾ teaspoon salt

¾ teaspoon freshly ground black pepper

1½ tablespoons all-purpose flour

½ cup finely chopped shallots or onion

2 tablespoons white dry vermouth

½ cup heavy cream

1 tablespoon chopped fresh tarragon or chives, for garnish

Rinse the morels briefly under cool running water and put them in a small bowl. Pour the tepid water over them and press a piece of aluminum foil on top, pushing it down into the mushrooms to keep them immersed in the water.

Divide the butter and oil between two skillets large enough to accommodate the scaloppine without overlapping. While you heat the butter and oil over high heat, sprinkle the scaloppine with about half the salt and pepper and dip them very lightly into the flour. Divide the scaloppine between the skillets and sauté them over high heat for about 1½ minutes on each side. Transfer to a serving plate.

Divide the shallots or onion between the two skillets and sauté for about 30 seconds. Add the mushrooms and soaking liquid, leaving behind any sand or dirt on the bottom. Boil for a few seconds to deglaze, then combine the mixture in one of the

skillets. Continue cooking, uncovered, over high heat for 4 to 5 minutes, or until the liquid is almost completely gone. Add the vermouth and cook for another minute. Add the cream and boil for a couple of minutes to reduce and thicken the sauce. Add the remaining salt and pepper and any liquid that has come out of the scaloppine.

Arrange 1 or 2 scaloppine on each of four warmed plates, then spoon the sauce and mushrooms on top of the scaloppine. Sprinkle on the tarragon or chives and serve.

Skirt Steak Grandma

Gloria's mother, originally from Puerto Rico, always rubbed lime juice on her steaks before cooking them and sprinkled lime juice liberally on the steaks after they were cooked. Her sauce included anchovies and garlic. This is a delicious interpretation of her recipe.

4 SERVINGS

4 skirt steaks (about 6 ounces each and about ¾ inch thick)

1 tablespoon fresh lime juice, plus more to sprinkle over the cooked steaks

½ teaspoon salt

½ teaspoon freshly ground black pepper

1 teaspoon good olive oil

1 can (2 ounces) anchovies in oil

2 teaspoons chopped garlic

2 tablespoons minced scallion

¼ cup water

Rub the steaks with the 1 tablespoon lime juice and sprinkle them with the salt and pepper 10 minutes before cooking.

Heat the olive oil and the oil from the anchovies in a large heavy skillet over high heat. When hot, add the steaks and cook them for about 1½ minutes on each side for medium rare, or for more or less time based on your own preferences.

Crush the anchovy fillets with the chopped garlic. When the steaks are ready, transfer them to a hot plate and set them aside to rest for a few minutes.

Meanwhile, add the anchovy-garlic paste and the scallions to the drippings in the pan and cook for about 30 seconds. Add the water and boil for 30 seconds. Pour over the steaks, sprinkle them with more lime juice, and serve.

CHILI CON CARNE WITH LETTUCE AND CHEESE

I used to have the chili con carne recipe from San Quentin Prison; the warden sent it to me in the 1960s when I worked at Howard Johnson's. Unfortunately, I lost it, but it was very similar to this coarsely textured chili of beef and red kidney beans. The amount and type of hot chile pepper—serrano, jalapeño, or the fiery habañero—is up to you and your family's preferences. I have added a little cocoa powder to give it a bit of depth, similar to the Mexican sauce called *mole*.

Making this dish in a pressure cooker (see page 119) requires less than 1 hour. I often serve it over crunchy iceberg or romaine lettuce leaves, with a sprinkling of grated Monterey Jack, mozzarella, or cheddar, a little cilantro, and some sliced onion on top.

To cook the chili conventionally, put all the ingredients in a large, heavy saucepan, bring to a boil, reduce the heat, and cook gently, covered, for 2 to 2½ hours, or until the beans are tender.

4 SERVINGS

¾ pound beef stew meat, cut into ½-inch pieces, or coarsely ground beef

8 ounces dried red kidney beans (about 1½ cups)

2 cups coarsely chopped onions

3 tablespoons coarsely chopped garlic

¾ cup coarsely chopped scallions

2 tablespoons tomato paste

1 can (14.5 ounces) diced tomatoes in sauce

1-2 serrano or jalapeño chile peppers, finely chopped

1½ tablespoons chili powder

1 tablespoon unsweetened cocoa powder

1½ teaspoons ground cumin

2 bay leaves

1 teaspoon dried oregano, preferably Mexican

2 tablespoons good olive oil

2 teaspoons salt

Freshly ground black pepper (optional)

3 cups cold water

Garnishes

8 large iceberg or romaine lettuce leaves

2 cups grated Monterey Jack, mozzarella, or cheddar cheese

1½ cups very finely sliced red onion, rinsed and drained

About 1½ cups loosely packed fresh cilantro leaves

Put all the ingredients except the garnishes in a 5- to 6-quart pressure cooker. Bring to a rolling boil, uncovered, over high heat. Mix well, secure the lid on the cooker, and cook over high heat until the gauge indicates that the pressure inside is on high. Reduce the heat to very low and cook for 50 minutes. Decompress the cooker according to the manufacturer's instructions. Open the lid, stir the chili, and add more salt and pepper, if desired. Remove the bay leaves.

To serve, arrange the lettuce leaves to resemble cups on four plates and ladle the chili into the leaves. Sprinkle on some cheese, red onion, and cilantro. Serve and enjoy.

SAUSAGE PATTIES WITH PUMPKIN SEEDS AND MUSHROOMS

This recipe reminds me of sausage links my mother served with mashed potatoes when I was a child. Extending the sausage meat with pumpkin seeds, mushrooms, and bread cuts down on the richness and makes it a great dish for serving with Cornmeal Mush, polenta, or grits for dinner. You can experiment with the sausage mixture; spinach, zucchini, and/or cheese would make great additions. For this recipe, I use the mild version, but if you prefer hot sausage, substitute it.

4 SERVINGS

1 pound sweet Italian sausage meat

2 tablespoons pumpkin seeds

1½ cups coarsely chopped white mushrooms (5–6 mushrooms)

1½ cups diced (¼-inch) white sandwich bread (about 2 slices)

1 tablespoon chopped fresh chives

1 teaspoon chopped garlic

½ teaspoon red pepper flakes (optional)

1 tablespoon good olive oil

Cornmeal Mush (page 151), polenta, or grits

In a medium bowl, mix the sausage meat, pumpkin seeds, mushrooms, bread, chives, garlic, and red pepper flakes, if using, together well with your hands. Divide into four patties, cover, and refrigerate or cook right away.

When you are ready to cook the patties, heat the olive oil in a large skillet. Sauté the patties over medium heat, covered most of the time, for 2½ to 3 minutes on each side. Let rest in the pan while you prepare Cornmeal Mush, polenta, or grits.

Spoon some mush, polenta, or grits on each of four plates, top with a patty, spoon some juices on top, and serve.

PORK MEDALLIONS WITH GRAPES IN POMEGRANATE SAUCE

Pork tenderloin is succulent, flavorful, and lean, delicious roasted whole or cut crosswise into medallions and sautéed. I accompany it with a sweet-sour sauce similar to what I would serve with venison, with pomegranate juice and chicken stock thickened with a little ketchup. Seedless grapes finish the dish nicely and shredded arugula gives it a special accent at the end, although you can use chopped chives or parsley instead, if you like.

4 SERVINGS

1 large pork tenderloin (about 1¼ pounds)

1 tablespoon unsalted butter

1 tablespoon good olive oil

¾ teaspoon salt

¾ teaspoon freshly ground black pepper

½ cup pomegranate juice

½ cup chicken stock, homemade (page 37), or low-salt canned chicken broth

2 tablespoons ketchup

1 cup small green seedless grapes

3 tablespoons dried cherries or cranberries

¼ cup shredded arugula

Trim the pork tenderloin of most of the fat and silverskin and cut it crosswise into 1-inch-thick medallions.

Preheat the oven to its lowest setting. Heat the butter and oil in a large, heavy skillet. Sprinkle the medallions with the salt and pepper. Arrange the medallions in a single layer in the skillet and cook them over high heat for about 2½ minutes on each side, or until lightly pink inside. Transfer the medallions to a plate and keep warm in the oven.

Add the pomegranate juice and chicken stock to the skillet, bring to a boil, reduce the heat to low, cover, and cook for 4 to 5 minutes. Add the ketchup, grapes, and cherries or cranberries and mix well. Boil for about 1 minute, or until the sauce is smooth and slightly thickened.

Arrange the medallions on four warm plates, coat with the sauce and grapes, and sprinkle with the shredded arugula. Serve.

STUFFED PORK TENDERLOIN ON GRAPE TOMATOES

For this recipe, I butterfly a pork tenderloin and stuff it with baby spinach and cheddar cheese. I roast it, slice, and serve on top of sautéed grape tomatoes. The stuffing can be prepared a few hours ahead. A couple of strips of aluminum foil wrapped around the tenderloin prevent it from opening during the browning; they are then removed when the pork goes into the oven.

4 SERVINGS

4 tablespoons good olive oil

½ cup chopped onion

1 package (7 ounces) prewashed baby spinach

¾ teaspoon salt

¾ teaspoon freshly ground black pepper

1 large pork tenderloin (about 1¼ pounds)

¾ cup grated cheddar cheese

1 box grape tomatoes (about 1½ pints)

Heat 2 tablespoons of the olive oil in a large skillet over high heat. Add the onion and cook for 1 minute. Add the spinach, pushing it down into the skillet, and ¼ teaspoon each of the salt and pepper. Cover and cook over medium heat for about 1½ minutes, until the spinach is wilted. Remove the lid and cook, uncovered, until the liquid from the spinach has evaporated. Transfer to a plate and let cool.

Trim the tenderloin of any fat and silverskin. To butterfly the tenderloin for stuffing, lay it flat on the cutting board so one end is close to you and the other end is near the top of the board. Holding your knife so the blade is parallel to the board, cut through the long side of the tenderloin, stopping when you are about ½ inch from the other side. Turn the tenderloin so the uncut side is closest to you and make another parallel cut below the first one, again stopping about ½ inch before you reach the other side. Open up the butterflied tenderloin and pound it a little to extend it to about 12 inches long by 7 inches wide.

Preheat the oven to 350 degrees. Arrange half the spinach mixture down the center of the butterflied tenderloin and top with the cheese. Add the rest of the spinach, fold in the sides, and roll the tenderloin back and forth to evenly distribute and encase the filling. Wrap 2 strips of aluminum foil, each 1 to 2 inches wide, around the tenderloin to secure the stuffing inside.

Heat the remaining 2 tablespoons oil in a large ovenproof nonstick skillet. Sprinkle the outside of the tenderloin with ¼ teaspoon each of the salt and pepper. Place the tenderloin carefully in the skillet and brown it, turning occasionally, for about 5 minutes. Carefully remove the foil strips from the tenderloin and bake in the oven for 10 minutes, when it will be slightly pink in the center. Transfer the tenderloin to a plate, cover, and keep warm in the oven while you prepare the tomatoes (the pork will continue to cook as it sits).

Add the tomatoes and the remaining ¼ teaspoon each salt and pepper to the skillet in which you browned the tenderloin and sauté over high heat for 1½ to 2 minutes, until just softened. Divide among four warm plates.

Slice the tenderloin crosswise into 8 medallions and arrange 2 slices in the middle of the tomatoes on each plate. Serve.

QUICK LAMB STEW

The pieces of lamb for this stew are pan-fried to rare or medium-rare at the last moment and served with the vegetable stew. The dish is finished with olives, capers, and a mixture of bread crumbs and almonds, a classic garnish in Arles, in the south of France. Some butcher shops and supermarkets will carry lamb stew meat; if yours does not, buy a piece of leg of lamb, trim it to remove all surrounding fat, and cut the meat into 2-inch chunks. Some parts of the leg are more tender than others, especially the part near the hip, which can be cut into steaks, while the lower part of the leg, near the shank, is better made into a long-simmering or pressure-cooked stew, like Lamb Curry (page 118).

4 TO 6 SERVINGS

1 cup cubed (about 1-inch) baguette

¼ cup whole almonds

2 teaspoons olive oil

½ cup chopped onion

1 cup diced (about 1-inch) white mushrooms

1 cup thinly sliced fennel (I slice mine with a Japanese vegetable slicer)

1 cup diced (about 1-inch) tomato

1 tablespoon chopped garlic

1½ teaspoons salt

½ cup water

3 tablespoons unsalted butter

2 pounds cubed (1½- to 2-inch pieces) lamb, all silverskin and fat removed

½ teaspoon freshly ground black pepper

About 20 pitted kalamata olives

Garnishes

1½ tablespoons drained capers

1 tablespoon minced fresh chives

Preheat the oven to 400 degrees. Spread the bread cubes and almonds on a cookie sheet and bake for about 8 minutes, or until brown and crusty. Cool for a few minutes, transfer to a heavy plastic bag, and crush coarsely by pounding with the base of a small pan or skillet.

Put the olive oil, onion, mushrooms, fennel, tomato, garlic, 1 teaspoon of the salt, and the water in a large saucepan and bring to a boil. Reduce the heat and simmer, covered, for 5 minutes.

When you are ready to finish the stew, heat the butter in a large nonstick skillet over high heat. Sprinkle the meat with the remaining ½ teaspoon salt and the

pepper. When the butter starts to turn brown, add the meat in a single layer to the skillet and brown for 6 to 7 minutes, turning so it sears nicely on all sides. Pour the mushroom mixture over the meat in the pan. Add the olives and toss. Transfer to a serving dish. Sprinkle with the capers, chives, and bread–almond crumbs. Serve.

LAMB CURRY

Winter is the time for stew and we often enjoy it at our house as a leisurely Sunday meal. One of my favorites is lamb curry, seasoned with garlic, curry powder, apple, banana, and coconut milk. Made in a pressure cooker, it is fast, easy, and can be prepared ahead. All the ingredients are combined in the cooker, and after the pressure is built up, the stew cooks in 25 minutes. Serve the curry, if you like, accompanied by Rice with Raisins (page 147). Beer is the perfect beverage.

To make this dish in a conventional pot, cook gently in an enameled cast-iron pot for 1¼ to 1½ hours, or until tender. Season, garnish, and serve as directed.

4 SERVINGS

2 pounds lamb from the leg shank area or shoulder, cut into about 16 large cubes

2 cups diced (1-inch) onions

3 tablespoons coarsely chopped garlic

1½ cups cubed (about 1½ inch) tomatoes

1 apple, cored but not peeled, cut into 1-inch pieces (about 1½ cups)

1 banana, peeled and sliced

1 tablespoon chopped jalapeño (about 1 small chile pepper), more or less depending on taste

1 cup coconut milk, well stirred

2½ tablespoons curry powder, plus more if desired

1 teaspoon ground cumin, plus more if needed

1 teaspoon salt, plus more if needed

2 bay leaves

½ cup fruity white wine

2 tablespoons instant flour, such as Wondra

Garnishes

Chopped fresh cilantro leaves

Chutney

Shredded unsweetened coconut

Roasted nuts

Put all the ingredients, except the flour and garnishes, in a pressure cooker. Sprinkle the flour on top and mix it well with the other ingredients. Bring to a boil over high heat. (This will take about 5 minutes.)

Secure the lid on the pressure cooker and cook the curry over high heat until the gauge indicates that the pressure is correct. Reduce the heat to very low to maintain the pressure at the correct level and cook for 25 minutes.

Decompress the pressure cooker according to manufacturer's instructions and remove the lid. Taste the stew for seasonings, adding more salt or spices, if you like. Remove the bay leaves.

Serve the stew, sprinkled with cilantro, with the chutney, shredded coconut, and roasted nuts on the side.

PRESSURE COOKERS

The pressure cooker is an essential piece of equipment at my house. My wife, Gloria, often cooks dried beans and makes stews in it. There are several makes and models on the market, all with slight differences, so follow the manufacturer's instructions when using them.

A pressure cooker is especially helpful at high elevations, where water boils at lower temperatures. (A couple of degrees are lost per 1,000 feet of elevation.) In Aspen, for example, water boils at around 196 degrees, a temperature that is often not high enough to break down the cellulose in beans and connective tissue in meat. A pressure cooker raises the boiling temperature to 250 degrees, rather than 212 degrees, the temperature at which water boils at sea level. This softens the fibers of meat, beans, and other foods, cooking and tenderizing the food much faster than conventional cooking methods.

An electric pressure cooker is also convenient. It has the advantage of a timer. When the contents reach the right pressure and temperature, the cooker shuts itself down, so you can leave for the day and the dish is ready when you get home.

LAMB BURGERS WITH FETA CHEESE AND YOGURT-CUCUMBER SAUCE

The Greeks, Turks, and other Middle Easterners cook more lamb than we do and use it in more imaginative ways. In this recipe, ground lamb is mixed with mushrooms, onion, garlic, and seasonings. It's formed into patties, and feta cheese is added. Some markets sell ground lamb, or you can buy lamb stew meat, leg of lamb, or shoulder lamb chops and grind them yourself. The lamb can have a little fat, but it should constitute no more than 8 percent of the meat.

The yogurt-cucumber sauce goes with any grilled meat or fish. Try to use Greek yogurt, which is creamier, thicker, and richer than regular yogurt.

4 SERVINGS

Yogurt-Cucumber Sauce
- 1 cucumber (about 10 ounces), peeled
- 1½ tablespoons chopped fresh mint
- 1 teaspoon chopped garlic
- ¾ teaspoon salt
- 1 tablespoon fresh lemon juice
- ½ teaspoon freshly ground black pepper
- 1 cup plain yogurt, preferably Greek

- 1 pound ground lamb
- 1 cup coarsely chopped cremini or white mushrooms
- ⅓ cup coarsely chopped onion
- 1 teaspoon finely chopped garlic
- ½ teaspoon ground cumin
- 1 teaspoon dried oregano, preferably Greek, or Mexican
- ½ cup crumbled (½-inch pieces) feta cheese
- 1 tablespoon olive oil
- ½ teaspoon salt
- ½ teaspoon freshly ground black pepper
- 2 pieces baguette, each about 3 inches long, split in half

For the sauce: Using the big holes of a box grater, grate the cucumber, turning it as you grate and stopping when you reach the seeds in the center and discarding them. You should have about 1½ cups grated cucumber. Mix it in a medium bowl with the rest of the sauce ingredients. (The yogurt sauce can be refrigerated for up to a week.)

Mix together in a medium bowl the ground lamb, mushrooms, onion, garlic, cumin, and oregano. Form the mixture into 4 patties, each about 1 inch thick. Make a shallow depression in the center of the top of each patty with your thumb and divide the cheese among the patties, piling it up in the slight depression. Carefully bring the outer edge of each patty over the cheese and press on it gently to cover and contain the cheese in the center of the patty.

Preheat the grill or heat a ridged grill pan or a large skillet over medium-high heat. Brush the patties with half the olive oil and sprinkle them with the salt and pepper. Brush the baguette halves on both sides with the remaining ½ tablespoon oil and place them on the hot grill, turning them once and then removing them when they are nicely browned on both sides. Arrange the patties on the grill and cook without pressing on them with the spatula for about 8 minutes, turning the patties occasionally to brown them well on both sides. They should be pink inside. Serve the open-face burgers on top of the grilled bread with the cucumber–yogurt sauce.

Vegetables

SKILLET BROCCOLI BITS

To me, the stems are the best part of the broccoli. They have to be peeled to remove the fibrous, tough outer skin, but they are firm, nutty, and buttery inside. Here both the peeled stems and the florets are cut into pieces and sautéed in a skillet. A little water is added at first and the broccoli is covered to start the cooking process. After it evaporates, the broccoli is finished uncovered.

This is especially good with Cod in Olive-Tomato Crust (page 82).

4 SERVINGS

1 bunch broccoli (about
   1¼ pounds)
¼ cup water
2 tablespoons good olive oil
½ teaspoon salt

Cut the broccoli florets off the stems and divide the florets into 1- to 1½-inch pieces. Peel the skin from the stems with a sharp knife or a vegetable peeler. Cut the peeled stems into 1-inch pieces.

Put the broccoli into a stainless-steel skillet and add the water, oil, and salt. Bring to a boil and cook, covered, over high heat for about 3 minutes. Remove the cover and cook over high heat for about 2 minutes, or until the water is gone and the broccoli is glazed and tender but still firm. Serve.

SAUTÉED JULIENNED ENDIVE

One of my favorite winter vegetables, Belgian endive is great in salads or braised or browned whole. Here the endive is sliced lengthwise by hand or on a slicer. The shreds are then sautéed in a skillet with oil and butter and a dash of sugar and salt until they brown and lightly caramelize. This is a perfect accompaniment to roasted or grilled meat or poultry.

4 SERVINGS

3 tablespoons unsalted butter

1 tablespoon canola oil

1½ pounds Belgian endive (5–8), washed and sliced lengthwise very thinly (8–9 cups)

¾ teaspoon salt

½ teaspoon freshly ground black pepper

1 teaspoon sugar

2 tablespoons minced fresh chives, for garnish

Heat the butter and oil in a large skillet. Add the sliced endive and sprinkle with the salt, pepper, and sugar. Cover and cook over high heat for 5 to 6 minutes, or until the endive releases most of its moisture. Uncover and cook over high heat for about 5 minutes longer, tossing the endive occasionally, until the moisture is gone and the endive browns lightly and caramelizes. Sprinkle with the chives and serve immediately. (The endive can be prepared up to 1 hour ahead and reheated in a microwave oven at serving time.)

SAUTÉED CURLY MUSTARD GREENS
WITH HOT SAUSAGE

I particularly like mustard greens in this recipe because of their spiciness, but you can also use kale, collard greens, or parsnip greens. Buy hot Italian bulk sausage for this dish.

4 SERVINGS

6 ounces hot Italian sausage meat, broken into pieces about the size of a hazelnut

½ cup chopped onion

1 pound curly mustard greens, cut into 4- to 5-inch chunks, washed, and dried in a salad spinner

½ teaspoon salt

½ teaspoon freshly ground black pepper

1 tablespoon extra-virgin olive oil

Put the sausage in a large nonstick skillet and cook it over medium heat for 5 minutes, or until the pieces are crisp. Add the onion and cook for 30 seconds. Increase the heat to high, add the greens and salt and pepper, and push the greens down into the pan so they soften a little. Cover and cook for 3 to 4 minutes, or until the greens are wilted, then uncover and cook over high heat for about 5 minutes longer to evaporate any moisture. When the greens are dry, serve them with a sprinkling of olive oil.

CRUNCHY KALE

When I was an apprentice in France, we often served fried parsley as a garnish. The parsley, usually the curly variety, was deep-fried in moderately hot peanut oil, drained, salted, and served, often as an accompaniment to fried fish. My friend Jean-Claude Szurdak has devised a way to get the same crunchy result by cooking curly kale in a low-temperature oven, a much leaner interpretation that is almost addictive. Claude's recipe produces crisp greens that are great as snacks, as a garnish for meat or fish, or simply crumbled over a salad.

4 TO 6 SERVINGS

½ pound curly kale, ribs removed and leaves broken into 2-inch pieces (5–6 loosely packed cups)

¼ teaspoon salt

1 tablespoon good olive oil

Preheat the oven to 250 degrees. Wash the greens, dry them well in a salad spinner, then toss them in a large bowl with the salt and olive oil. Place a wire cooling rack on a cookie sheet and spread the greens out in a single layer on the rack. Bake, without stirring, for 20 to 25 minutes. The leaves should remain a bright deep green; if they begin to brown, they will taste slightly bitter. Store in an airtight container and use as needed.

STEW OF PEAS AND CARROTS

This is the type of vegetable stew my mother used to make when I was a child. She always made a roux as the base for the vegetables, which gave the stew a special taste that will always be part of my food memory.

4 TO 6 SERVINGS

2 tablespoons unsalted butter

1 cup chopped onion

½ cup minced scallions

1 tablespoon all-purpose flour

1¼ cups water

1½ cups peeled and diced (½-inch) carrots

¾ teaspoon salt

½ teaspoon freshly ground black pepper

¼ teaspoon dried thyme

1 package (16 ounces) frozen petite peas

Melt the butter in a saucepan. When hot, add the onion and scallions and sauté over medium to high heat for about 2 minutes. Add the flour and mix well. Stir in the water and add the carrots, salt, pepper, and thyme. Bring the mixture to a boil, cover, and boil for 5 minutes.

Add the frozen peas to the saucepan and bring the mixture to a boil again. Cover, reduce the heat to low, and bring back to a boil (it will take 4 to 5 minutes). Boil gently for about 3 minutes, or until the peas are as tender as you like. Serve.

PEAS, MUSHROOMS, AND ENDIVE

This stew features an unusual combination of vegetables. Petite peas are the small ones in the pods, which are sweeter and more tender than the starchy large peas. The slight bitterness of the endive and the earthy taste and firm texture of the mushrooms lend complexity to this dish.

4 SERVINGS

2 teaspoons peanut or canola oil

1 cup coarsely chopped white mushrooms

1 large Belgian endive, cut crosswise into 1-inch slices (about 2 cups)

2 cups (about 8 ounces) frozen petite peas

½ teaspoon salt

½ teaspoon freshly ground black pepper

1½ tablespoons unsalted butter

Heat the oil in a large skillet. When hot, add the mushrooms and endive. Cover and cook over medium to high heat for 4 to 5 minutes, stirring occasionally, until the moisture is gone and the mixture starts sizzling. Add the peas, salt, and pepper, uncover, and continue cooking for about 2 minutes, or until the peas soften and get hot and tender. Add the butter and cook for another minute while tossing the mixture. Serve.

FRICASSEE OF BRUSSELS SPROUTS AND BACON

For many years I cooked brussels sprouts in salted water and then sautéed them whole or halved in butter, seasoning them with a little salt and pepper. They were good, but not extraordinary. This recipe, however, gives fantastic results. I slice the sprouts raw in my food processor and sauté them with bacon bits. The whole process takes fewer than 10 minutes.

When buying brussels sprouts, make sure they are firm, bright green, and not damaged. The root end is usually discolored and it should be trimmed or removed, along with any damaged leaves. When buying your sprouts, remember to buy enough so the trimmed weight is about 1 pound: 1¼ pounds should do it.

4 SERVINGS

1 pound trimmed and cleaned brussels sprouts

4 slices bacon, cut crosswise into ¼-inch pieces (about ¾ cup)

2 tablespoons good olive oil

½ teaspoon salt

½ teaspoon freshly ground black pepper

Using the slicing blade on your food processor, cut the brussels sprouts into slices about ¼ inch thick. (You should have about 5 cups.)

Scatter the bacon pieces in a large skillet, add the oil, cover, and cook over high heat for 2 to 3 minutes, until the pieces are crisp and brown and most of the fat is rendered. Add the sliced sprouts, salt, and pepper, cover, and cook for 1 to 2 minutes to soften the sprouts. Uncover and cook over high heat, tossing occasionally, for about 2 minutes, until the sprouts are tender but still a bit firm. Serve.

RAGOUT OF BROCCOLINI,
BEANS, AND SAUSAGE

White beans, sausage, and broccoli are a classic Mediterranean combination. Instead of broccoli, I use broccolini, because it is more tender and the stems don't need peeling. Preparing the dish with canned cannellini beans makes it a cinch.

4 SERVINGS

2 tablespoons good olive oil, plus more for drizzling (optional)

½ cup chopped onion

6 ounces hot Italian sausage meat

1 can (15.5 ounces) cannellini beans

1 small bunch (8–10 ounces) broccolini

2 teaspoons chopped garlic

¼ teaspoon salt, plus more if needed

⅛ teaspoon red pepper flakes

Grated Parmesan cheese (optional)

Pour the oil into a large skillet or saucepan and add the onion and sausage. Cook over high heat for 2 to 3 minutes, breaking the sausage meat into small pieces with a fork or spoon. Add the liquid from the can of beans and bring to a boil.

Meanwhile, wash and cut the broccolini tops into 1-inch pieces and the stems into ½-inch pieces. Add to the pan with the garlic, salt, and red pepper flakes and return to a boil. Cover and boil gently for 4 to 5 minutes, or until the broccolini is tender but still a little crunchy.

Add the beans, mix well, and return to a boil. Boil, uncovered, for 2 to 3 minutes to blend the flavors together. Taste and add more salt if needed. Serve as is, or sprinkle with the Parmesan cheese and extra oil.

SPINACH, MACADAMIA NUTS, AND RAISINS

Crunchy, buttery macadamia nuts and raisins give a hint of sweetness and tartness to this spinach. Small, tender leaves need only a couple of minutes in the skillet. If your spinach leaves are large, remove the tough stems before cooking.

4 SERVINGS

2 tablespoons good olive oil

½ cup macadamia nut pieces

1 pound small spinach leaves or larger spinach leaves with big stems removed, washed but still damp

¼ cup raisins

½ teaspoon salt

½ teaspoon freshly ground black pepper

Heat the oil in a large skillet over high heat. Add the nuts and sauté for 1 to 2 minutes to brown the nuts lightly. Add the damp spinach, pressing it down into the pan, and sprinkle the raisins, salt, and pepper on top. Cover and cook for about 2 minutes. The spinach will start to wilt. Stir with tongs so the nuts do not burn underneath and the raisins, salt, and pepper are distributed throughout.

After the spinach has wilted, cook, uncovered, for about 1 minute longer to cook away most of the remaining moisture. Serve.

BUTTERNUT SQUASH SAUTÉ

I always got a kick out of bringing the seeds from butternut squash to my brother, Roland, in France, where this variety does not exist. The butternuts were a big hit with his neighbors when he picked them from his garden.

I often puree the squash for soups and gratins and sometimes split it in half and bake it. For this recipe, I prepare it the way we make potato sautés in France, adding some cider to coat the squash pieces with a caramelized glaze. It makes a great dish for the Thanksgiving and Christmas holidays. To save yourself some work, buy peeled and seeded butternut squash if it's available in the produce department of your supermarket; it's worth the extra money.

4 SERVINGS

1 small (about 1½ pounds) butternut squash

1 cup diced (¾-inch) onion

1 tablespoon canola or peanut oil

3 tablespoons unsalted butter

¾ teaspoon salt

½ teaspoon sugar

1 cup apple cider

2 teaspoons cider vinegar

2 tablespoons chopped fresh parsley leaves, for garnish

Trim the squash at both ends and cut off the neck (the part without seeds). Peel the squash at least twice with a good vegetable peeler to ensure that you remove the skin and all the green flesh under it. Cut the squash in half and remove and discard the seeds. Cut the peeled squash into a ¾-inch dice. You should have about 4 cups.

Put all the ingredients except the parsley into a large skillet, preferably nonstick. Cover, bring to a boil, and boil over high heat for about 6 minutes, until the squash pieces are somewhat tender. Continue cooking, uncovered, stirring occasionally, until the liquid is completely gone. Cook for a few minutes longer, stirring and shaking the pan to prevent the squash from burning, until the squash pieces are caramelized to your liking. Sprinkle with the parsley and serve.

PUMPKIN GRATIN

The only way I ate pumpkin as a child was in a savory gratin, so the first time I had it in the United States—sweet, in a pie—I thought it was a mistake. I've come to love pumpkin pie and I still enjoy pumpkin in the gratin of my youth. The combination of Swiss cheese, eggs, and cream comes together into something like a smooth and creamy soufflé, capturing the flavors of fall. Canned pumpkin speeds things up.

4 SERVINGS

1 can (15.5 ounces) 100% pure pumpkin puree (not pumpkin pie filling)

3 large eggs

1 cup heavy cream

¾ cup grated Swiss cheese

¾ teaspoon salt

½ teaspoon freshly ground black pepper

1 teaspoon unsalted butter

1 tablespoon grated Parmesan cheese

Preheat the oven to 350 degrees. Spoon the pumpkin puree into a food processor and add the eggs, cream, cheese, salt, and pepper. Process for 10 to 15 seconds to combine.

Coat a 6-cup gratin dish with the butter. Fill the dish with the pumpkin mixture. Sprinkle the Parmesan cheese on top and bake for 35 to 45 minutes, until set and lightly browned on top. Serve.

CORN PARFAIT

A parfait is a smooth creamy dessert and this savory recipe is rich-tasting and smooth as well, hence the name. Corn dishes are always best in their season, with ears picked fresh from the garden, yet supermarkets generally have pretty good corn most of the year. This dish is a great addition to roast meat or grilled fish, as well as being a good first course for dinner or main course for lunch. The parfait is always better when slightly wet and undercooked in the center.

4 SERVINGS

1 teaspoon unsalted butter, softened

4 ears corn, husked

2 tablespoons all-purpose flour

3 large eggs

1 teaspoon salt

½ teaspoon freshly ground black pepper

1½ cups half-and-half

1 tablespoon grated Parmesan cheese

Coat a 4- to 5-cup gratin dish with the butter. Preheat the oven to 375 degrees.

Cut the kernels off the ears of corn and put them in a food processor with the flour, eggs, salt, and pepper. Process until well pureed. Add the half-and-half and process for another 5 to 10 seconds. Pour into the buttered dish and sprinkle the Parmesan cheese on top.

Bake for about 25 minutes, or until just barely set in the center, puffy, and nicely browned. Serve. (The parfait is best served immediately, but you can make it 1 to 2 hours ahead and reheat it in the oven or the microwave.)

POTATOES, RICE, PASTA, PIZZA, AND BREAD

FLUFFY MASHED POTATOES

The mashed potatoes that my aunt from Valence made were better than any others. She told me once that the reason was the clove of unpeeled garlic she cooked with the potatoes. When she pushed the potatoes through a food mill or ricer, the garlic pulp contributed just a faint flavor. She always added butter to her mashed potatoes and made them with milk, never cream. Whisking the mixture makes it fluffy, creating what we call *pommes mousseline* in French. Serve with Roasted Split Chicken with Mustard Crust (page 99).

4 SERVINGS

1 pound potatoes, preferably Yukon Gold or Red Bliss, peeled

1 large garlic clove, unpeeled

2½ tablespoons unsalted butter, softened

⅔ cup milk, heated in a microwave oven to warm, plus 2–3 more tablespoons milk if not serving the potatoes immediately

½ teaspoon salt

¼ teaspoon freshly ground black pepper

Put the potatoes, garlic, and 3 cups water in a medium saucepan and bring to a boil over high heat. Reduce the heat and boil gently for about 25 minutes, or until the potatoes are fork-tender. Drain and push the potatoes through a food mill or ricer. (A food processor will make them gooey.) Add the butter and mix well with a wooden spoon until incorporated. Add about ⅓ cup of the milk and mix well with the spoon. Pour in the remaining ⅓ cup milk and add the salt and pepper. Using a whisk, whip the potatoes for 15 to 20 seconds, until they are fluffy and very smooth.

If the potatoes are not to be served immediately, smooth the top and pour 2 to 3 tablespoons milk on the potatoes to keep them moist. At serving time, stir the milk into the potatoes, reheat, and serve.

POTATO GRATIN WITH CREAM

I often serve boiled potatoes, with or without the skin, as an accompaniment to meat or fish. When I have some potatoes left over, I turn them into this sinfully rich potato gratin.

4 SERVINGS

1 teaspoon unsalted butter, softened

About 1 pound boiled potatoes

¼ teaspoon grated nutmeg

½ teaspoon salt

½ teaspoon freshly ground black pepper

1 cup heavy cream

¼ cup grated Parmesan cheese

Coat a 4- to 6-cup gratin dish with butter. Preheat the oven to 400 degrees. If using cooked potatoes with skin, peel off the skin. Cut the potatoes into ¼-inch-thick slices. Arrange in the gratin dish. Sprinkle with the nutmeg, salt, and pepper and pour on the cream. Using a fork or spoon, press down on the top of the potato slices so they are level and wet with the cream.

Cover the top generously with the cheese and bake for 20 minutes, until nicely browned, crusty, and hot. Serve.

CRIQUES (POTATO PANCAKES)
ON MESCLUN SALAD

One of my sister-in-law's specialties was *criques,* crisp potato pancakes. She grated the potatoes on a box grater. In this recipe, I speed things up by mixing the raw potatoes, onion, and most of the other ingredients in a food processor.

The pancakes are best served right out of the skillet, but if you want to make them ahead, they recrisp nicely when reheated in a hot oven just before serving. My pancakes are about 4 inches in diameter, but you can make them smaller for hors d'oeuvres, or larger and topped with some sour cream and smoked salmon for an elegant main course.

4 SERVINGS (ABOUT 18)

2 cups peeled and cubed (about 1-inch) potatoes

1 cup cubed (1-inch) onion

2 garlic cloves, peeled

2 large eggs

2 tablespoons potato starch (found in the kosher section of supermarkets) or all-purpose flour

½ teaspoon baking powder

½ teaspoon salt

½ teaspoon freshly ground black pepper

¼ cup minced scallions

Peanut or canola oil, to sauté the pancakes

Mesclun Salad

4 cups mesclun salad greens

1 tablespoon extra-virgin olive oil

1 tablespoon red wine vinegar

Dash salt and freshly ground black pepper

Put the potatoes, onion, garlic, eggs, potato starch or flour, baking powder, salt, and pepper in a food processor. Process for about 30 seconds to combine the ingredients well. The texture will be grainy. Stir in the scallions.

Heat about 3 tablespoons oil in a large nonstick skillet over high heat. When it is hot, add about ¼ cup batter, spreading it out to form a pancake about 4 inches in diameter. Repeat this to have 4 pancakes cooking side by side in the pan. (If using a smaller pan, make multiple batches.) Cook the pancakes for about 3 minutes on each side over medium to high heat. They should be well browned.

Transfer the pancakes to a wire rack so they don't get mushy on the underside. Repeat making pancakes until all the batter is used. Serve. (The *criques* can be made 1 to 2 hours ahead and reheated on a baking sheet in a 425-degree oven for about 5 minutes before serving.)

For the mesclun salad: Toss the greens in a bowl with the olive oil, vinegar, and salt and pepper. Divide among four plates and arrange the *criques* on top.

Variation: As a special treat, serve the *criques* with caviar and sour cream.

RICE WITH RAISINS

Golden raisins bring an appealingly chewy texture to a dish that makes a perfect companion for Lamb Curry (page 118).

4 SERVINGS

1 tablespoon canola oil

½ cup chopped onion

1¼ cups long-grain white rice

¼ cup golden raisins

2½ cups water

½ teaspoon salt

¼ teaspoon freshly ground black pepper

Heat the oil in a medium saucepan over high heat. Add the onion and cook for about 30 seconds. Add the rice and raisins and mix well. Add the water, salt, and pepper and bring to a boil, stirring a couple of times. Cover, reduce the heat to very low, and cook gently for 20 minutes, or until the rice is tender. Serve.

RISOTTO WITH BROCCOLI STEMS

Risotto never fails to please as a first course, and if garnishes are added it can be varied ad infinitum. My wife, Gloria, makes risotto with Japanese sushi rice with great success, but for this recipe I use Italian short-grain rice.

Broccoli stems are often discarded by cooks because of their thick, fibrous skin, but a quick peeling makes them deliciously edible. I keep the florets for another recipe and use only the stems here. Depending on the size of the stalks, you'll need 3 or 4 good-sized stems to get enough broccoli for this recipe.

I cook my risotto, covered, to the halfway point (about 8 minutes) in about the same amount of chicken stock as I have rice. Then I finish it uncovered, adding small quantities of liquid until I achieve the right consistency and degree of doneness. This is the same way risotto is often made in restaurants: it is already partially cooked so it can be finished portion by portion in 8 to 10 minutes when the order comes from the dining room.

4 SERVINGS

1 cup water

3–4 broccoli stems, fibrous outer skin peeled, cut into ½-inch dice (about 2 cups)

3–4 white mushrooms

2 tablespoons olive oil

¼ cup chopped onion

¼ cup finely minced scallions

1 cup Italian short-grain (risotto) rice

¾ teaspoon salt

2¼ cups chicken stock, homemade (page 37), or turkey stock, or low-salt canned chicken broth

2 tablespoons butter

¼ cup grated Parmesan cheese, plus more for the table

Bring the water to a boil in a large saucepan. Add the diced broccoli stems, bring to a boil, and cook for about 2 minutes, or until they are tender but still crunchy. Drain and set aside. Wash and cut the mushrooms into ½-inch-thick slices. Pile up the slices and cut (julienne) them into ¼-inch sticks. You should have about 1 cup.

Heat the olive oil in a saucepan over high heat and add the onion and scallions. Cook for about 30 seconds. Add the mushroom julienne and the rice. Mix well and stir in the salt and 1¼ cups of the stock. Bring to a boil, stir well, cover, reduce the heat to low, and cook for about 8 minutes. Uncover. The liquid should be completely absorbed. If not, continue cooking until it is dry. (The risotto can be prepared to this point up to 2 hours ahead.)

When you're ready to finish the risotto, heat the mixture over medium-high heat until it is sizzling, add ¼ cup of the remaining stock, and stir well. Continue stirring occasionally until this liquid is absorbed and the mixture starts sizzling again, which should take about 2 minutes. Repeat this procedure 3 more times, adding ¼ cup stock each time. Add the butter, cheese, and broccoli stems at the end of the cooking, stirring them in for 1 to 2 minutes, until the risotto is creamy but the grains of rice are still firm to the bite in the center. Serve right away on very hot plates, passing the Parmesan at the table.

CORNMEAL MUSH

What Italians call polenta and we call hominy grits in the southern United States is known as cornmeal in most of the U.S. and masa harina in Mexico. It is either yellow or white, depending on the corn. Each of these products has slightly different properties, but they can be served interchangeably as side dishes. It's handy to have some cornmeal in the pantry. Cornmeal Mush is delicious served with any fish or meat dish—and particularly as an accompaniment for Sausage Patties with Pumpkin Seeds and Mushrooms (page 109). If serving with the sausage patties, place a patty in the middle of each mound and sprinkle the sausage cooking juices on top.

4 SERVINGS

4 cups water
½ teaspoon salt
1 cup minute or instant yellow or white cornmeal

Bring the water to a boil in a medium saucepan and add the salt. Add the cornmeal and stir it in with a whisk to prevent lumping. Bring back to a boil, then reduce the heat to low and cook, partially covered, according to the package instructions, stirring occasionally. At serving time, mound on warm plates and serve immediately.

MIDDLE EASTERN COUSCOUS
WITH SAFFRON

In the last few years, a larger, pebblelike variety of couscous, known variously as Israeli, Middle Eastern, Moroccan, or Italian couscous, has appeared on the market. Like instant couscous, it is made of semolina, but its grains are much larger, about the size of peppercorns.

For this recipe, I cook the couscous covered for about 10 minutes and then uncover it and cook it for a few minutes longer, stirring occasionally, to produce loose, soft, tender grains that are neither sticky nor soupy. I season the dish with onion and saffron and add pumpkin seeds for crunch.

4 SERVINGS

2 tablespoons good olive oil

2/3 cup finely chopped onion

1/4 cup pumpkin seeds

About 1 teaspoon crushed saffron pistils

1 cup Israeli couscous

1½ cups chicken stock, homemade (page 37), or low-salt canned chicken broth

1/4 teaspoon salt

1/4 teaspoon freshly ground black pepper

4 sprigs fresh tarragon or parsley, for garnish

Heat the oil in a medium saucepan over high heat and add the onion, pumpkin seeds, and saffron. Cook for 1 to 2 minutes, then add the couscous and mix well. Add the chicken stock, salt, and pepper, mix well, and bring to a boil. Reduce the heat to very low, cover, and cook for 10 minutes. Uncover and cook over medium heat, stirring occasionally, for 2 to 3 minutes longer to dry the grains and make them fluffy. Serve garnished with the herb sprigs.

VEGETABLE COUSCOUS

I have prepared and enjoyed couscous for decades. This granulated, dry wheat semolina is quick to prepare at the last minute. A perfect accompaniment to roasted or grilled meat or fish, vegetable couscous is also good on its own for a light lunch with a salad or an omelet. Cook the vegetables no more than an hour ahead; otherwise, the green vegetables, like broccoli or spinach, start to turn brown or yellow.

You can change the variety of vegetables here based on what you have on hand or on what is available at the market.

4 SERVINGS

3 tablespoons good olive oil

½ cup coarsely chopped onion

1 cup diced (1-inch) white mushrooms

1 cup diced (1-inch) broccoli

1 cup diced (1-inch) tomato

2 cups (lightly packed) baby spinach

1 cup canned chickpeas, drained

¾ teaspoon salt

¾ teaspoon freshly ground black pepper

¾ cup chicken stock, homemade (page 37), or low-salt canned chicken broth

1¼ cups instant couscous

Heat the oil in a medium saucepan over high heat and add the onion. Cook for about 1 minute, stirring occasionally. Add the mushrooms, broccoli, tomato, spinach, chickpeas, salt, pepper, and chicken stock. Cover and bring to a rolling boil. It will take 5 to 6 minutes to come to a boil. Boil for 1 minute.

Stir in the couscous. Bring back to a light boil, remove from the heat, cover, and let stand for about 5 minutes. Fluff with a fork and serve.

RATATOUILLE WITH PENNE

Ratatouille, the classic vegetable stew of Provence, is featured in all the small restaurants along its coast. Vegetables for ratatouille are usually prepared separately and not combined until the end. Here everything is cooked together. I don't bother to peel the eggplant, but do so if you wish. I recommend Japanese eggplants for this dish. Long and thin, they are firmer and have fewer seeds than regular eggplants.

Ratatouille is generally served on its own, at room temperature, sprinkled with the best-quality olive oil, olives, and parsley (see the note on page 156). I use it as a pasta sauce, tossing it with cooked penne before garnishing it with olive oil, olives, grated Parmesan cheese, and parsley or basil.

4 SERVINGS

Ratatouille

- 1 long Japanese eggplant or small regular eggplant (about 10 ounces), cut into 1-inch pieces
- 2 small firm zucchini (about ½ pound total), cut into ¾-inch cubes
- 2 cubanelle or long Italian peppers (about ½ pound total), seeded and cut into 1-inch pieces
- 2 cups cubed (¾-inch) onions
- 2 tablespoons coarsely chopped garlic
- 1 can (14.5 ounces) diced tomatoes in sauce
- 2 teaspoons salt
- ¼ cup olive oil

Penne

- Salt
- ¾ pound penne (I use small penne mezzanine)
- ¾ teaspoon freshly ground black pepper
- 3 tablespoons olive oil
- ½ cup small pitted oil-cured black olives
- ¼ cup grated Parmesan cheese, plus more for the table
- A few fresh basil or parsley leaves, for garnish

For the ratatouille: Put all the ingredients in a large saucepan and bring to a boil over high heat. Mix well, reduce the heat to low, cover, and cook gently for 30 minutes. If the mixture still has a lot of liquid, reduce it by boiling, uncovered, for 3 to 4 minutes. Cool to room temperature. You will have about 5 cups.

For the penne: Bring 3 quarts salted water to a boil in a large pot. Add the penne and stir it in well, so it doesn't stick together. Return to a boil, stirring occasionally, and cook for 10 to 12 minutes, or until it is cooked to your liking.

Meanwhile, combine the ratatouille, ¾ teaspoon salt, pepper, and olive oil in a large glass bowl and microwave for a couple of minutes to warm it through. Drain the pasta and add it to the ratatouille in the bowl. Sprinkle on the olives and the cheese and mix well. Divide among four hot plates and garnish with the basil and grated cheese. Pass more at the table.

Note: To serve the ratatouille on its own, spoon it into a serving dish, drizzle on a little extra-virgin olive oil, sprinkle with ¼ cup pitted oil–cured black olives or kalamata olives, and garnish with 2 tablespoons coarsely chopped fresh basil or parsley.

Spaghetti with Fresh Tomato and Anchovy Sauce

Pasta is often the entrée of choice at our dinner table when we decide on a menu at the last moment. I particularly like it with fresh sauces made with tomatoes, mushrooms, and herbs. I put all the sauce ingredients in a bowl and warm them in my microwave oven before mixing them with the hot pasta. I always add some of the hot cooking water to the sauce. When the pasta and sauce are tossed together, the pasta absorbs the water. Be sure to serve your pasta on very hot plates with extra Parmesan cheese.

4 SERVINGS

Salt

4-5 baby bella or white mushrooms

1 cup frozen petite peas

2 cups diced (½-inch) tomatoes

1½ tablespoons chopped garlic

3 tablespoons chopped anchovies, with their oil

¾ teaspoon red pepper flakes

¼ cup good olive oil

3 tablespoons grated Parmesan cheese, plus more to pass at the table

1 pound thin spaghetti, or another pasta of your liking

¾ cup (loosely packed) fresh cilantro leaves

Bring 3 quarts salted water to a boil in a large pot. Meanwhile, cut the mushrooms into thin slices. Pile the slices together and cut them into thin strips (julienne). You should have 1½ cups. Combine them in a large glass bowl with the peas.

Add the diced tomatoes, garlic, and anchovies with their oil to the bowl. Sprinkle on the red pepper flakes, 1 teaspoon salt, olive oil, and grated Parmesan cheese. Mix well.

Add the pasta to the boiling water and cook for 7 to 8 minutes, or until done to your liking. Meanwhile, heat the tomato mixture in the microwave oven for about 2 minutes. When the pasta is cooked, ladle out about ¾ cup of the hot pasta water before draining the pasta and mix it into the sauce in the bowl to warm it up.

Drain the pasta and add it to the sauce along with the cilantro. Toss well for 15 or 20 seconds, then divide among four hot plates. Serve immediately, with extra grated Parmesan cheese.

RIGATONI WITH LETTUCE AND EGGPLANT

My wife, Gloria, loves eggplant, so I prepare it in a variety of ways throughout the year. Eggplant can absorb a great deal of oil when fried, but baking it makes it possible to use far less. Combined with wilted lettuce—anything from Boston to escarole to romaine—the eggplant is mixed with pasta, anchovies, and garlic. This dish can also be prepared with farfalle, penne, or fusilli; I make it here with rigatoni, a large, hearty pasta.

4 SERVINGS

1 eggplant (about 1¼ pounds)
Salt
¾ pound rigatoni
¼ cup good olive oil
¼ cup sliced garlic
½ teaspoon red pepper flakes
6 cups torn lettuce (iceberg, Boston, escarole, and/or romaine)
1 jar (3.5 ounces) anchovy fillets in oil
¼ cup grated Parmesan cheese, plus more for the table

Preheat the oven to 400 degrees. Peel the eggplant and cut it into 1-inch pieces. Line a baking sheet with a reusable nonstick mat or spray with nonstick cooking spray. Spread the eggplant pieces in one layer on the baking sheet and sprinkle the pieces with ¾ teaspoon salt. Bake for about 20 minutes, until the eggplant is soft. Set aside.

Bring 3 quarts salted water to a boil in a large pot and stir the rigatoni into the boiling water. Cook for 15 to 16 minutes, until done to your liking.

Meanwhile, heat the olive oil in a large skillet over high heat. Add the garlic and pepper flakes and cook for about 1 minute. Add the lettuce. Mix well, cover, and cook for about 3 minutes, stirring occasionally. Add the eggplant and ½ teaspoon salt and mix well. Cut the anchovies into ½-inch pieces and add them along with their oil to the skillet. Mix well.

Remove 1 cup of the pasta cooking water and add it to the eggplant mixture. Drain the pasta and combine it with the eggplant. Sprinkle on the Parmesan cheese and mix well. Divide among four hot plates and serve immediately with extra grated Parmesan cheese.

ORECCHIETTE WITH FENNEL AND TUNA

This main dish was inspired by Sicilian *pasta con sarda,* or pasta with sardines. My version, with tuna instead of sardines, is a cinch to make. I cut the fennel into very thin slices with a small Japanese vegetable slicer.

4 SERVINGS

Salt

⅓ cup olive oil

1½ cups chopped onions

3 tablespoons pignoli nuts

1½ tablespoons chopped garlic

2 tablespoons golden raisins

¼ cup chopped fresh parsley

1 teaspoon freshly ground black pepper

2 cans (6 ounces each) tuna packed in water

1 fennel bulb (about ¾ pound), cut into very thin slices

3 tablespoons water

1 pound orecchiette (or a similar type) pasta

Grated Parmesan cheese (optional)

Bring a pot of salted water to a boil.

Meanwhile, heat the olive oil in a large skillet over high heat until hot but not smoking. Add the onions and pignoli nuts and sauté for 1 minute. Add the garlic, raisins, parsley, 1½ teaspoons salt, and pepper. Crumble the tuna into 1-inch pieces, add it with its juice to the skillet, and cook for 20 seconds. Add the fennel and water. Bring to a boil, cover, and cook for 2 to 3 minutes, until most of the water is gone and the fennel is tender. Transfer the mixture to a bowl large enough to hold the cooked pasta.

Add the pasta to the boiling water. Return the water to a boil and boil the pasta for about 8 minutes, or until done to your liking.

Add ½ cup of the pasta water to the tuna and fennel mixture in the bowl and drain the pasta. Add the pasta to the bowl, toss well, and serve with Parmesan cheese, if desired.

CHORIZO, MUSHROOM, AND CHEESE PIZZA

I keep ready-made pizza crusts (such as Boboli) in my refrigerator or freezer in case people show up unexpectedly for drinks. I also stock sausages in my freezer and cheese in my refrigerator to use as toppings.

These pizzas can also be made with tortillas, which require only about 10 minutes to cook, and with different toppings, among them sliced tomato, Gruyère cheese, and zucchini—whatever you have on hand. I like assertive cheeses on my pizza, so I often combine some leftover blue with Camembert and/or Brie, Reblochon, or St. Albray. Serve with a green salad.

4 SERVINGS

1 ready-made 12-inch pizza crust

2 tablespoons good olive oil

⅔ cup sliced onion

1 cup coarsely chopped (¼-inch) chorizo sausage

⅔ cup coarsely chopped white mushrooms (4–5 mushrooms)

1 cup thinly sliced green bell pepper strips

2 tablespoons thinly sliced garlic

¼ teaspoon salt

¼ teaspoon freshly ground black pepper

About 1½ cups sliced cheese, such as St. Albray, fontina, Camembert, mozzarella, Beaufort, or a mixture of these

Preheat the oven to 400 degrees. Brush the bottom of the pizza crust with a little of the oil. Place the crust on a cookie sheet, sprinkle the onion on top, and evenly distribute the chorizo, mushrooms, bell pepper, and sliced garlic on the crust. Sprinkle with the salt and pepper and top with the cheese. Sprinkle on the remaining oil.

Bake for about 20 minutes, or until well browned and crisp. Cut into wedges and serve.

SMOKED SALMON PIZZA

I love to make pizza with my own dough, as well as with lavash, tortillas, pita bread, and naan, a wonderful Indian flatbread now available in most markets. I crisp the flatbreads in the oven or in a skillet on top of the stove, then top them with smoked salmon, which is available in different styles from Scotland, Ireland, and Canada at the deli counter.

This smoked salmon pizza is great cut into bite-size pieces for hors d'oeuvres.

4 TO 6 FIRST-COURSE SERVINGS

1 tablespoon extra-virgin olive oil

1 lavash (12 by 9 inches), or 2 naan flatbreads (8 ounces total, about 9 by 7 inches each)

½ cup sour cream

2 teaspoons bottled horseradish, drained

½ cup thinly sliced red onion

8 ounces sliced smoked salmon

2 tablespoons drained capers

Freshly ground black pepper

¼ cup fresh cilantro leaves

Preheat the oven to 400 degrees. Brush a baking sheet with the oil and turn the lavash or naan in the oil to coat the bread on both sides. Bake for 8 to 10 minutes, until the bread is crusty and brown. Let cool to lukewarm.

Mix the sour cream and horseradish in a small bowl. Spread on the bread and sprinkle half the onion over the sour cream mixture. Arrange the smoked salmon slices on top. Sprinkle the capers over the salmon and add the remaining onion and some freshly ground black pepper. Finally, sprinkle with the cilantro leaves. Cut the pizza into wedges or slices and serve.

TIBETAN FLATBREAD

I first sampled a version of this bread in a Tibetan restaurant. The dough is similar to that for Irish soda bread, but unlike soda bread, which has to cook in the oven, this one is quickly cooked in a nonstick skillet.

You can add scallions, fresh or dried herbs, chopped mushrooms, or other vegetables to the dough for a variation.

4 SERVINGS

1½ cups all-purpose flour

1 teaspoon baking powder

⅓ teaspoon salt

1 cup water, plus about 2 tablespoons more for steaming the bread

1 tablespoon olive oil

Combine the flour, baking powder, and salt in a medium bowl. Add the 1 cup water and mix together with a sturdy rubber spatula to create a thick, gooey dough.

Spread the oil in a cold 12-inch nonstick skillet. Add the dough to the skillet. Dip the spatula into the oil in the skillet and use it to press on the dough to flatten it in the skillet. (The oil will prevent the dough from sticking to the spatula.) Add the 2 tablespoons water to create a bit of steam and get the bread cooking. Cover and place over medium-high heat for about 10 minutes. The water should be gone and the dough should be frying at this point. Reduce the heat and, using a fork, turn the bread over. Cover and cook for another 5 minutes. Uncover and set aside to cool a little in the skillet. Cut into wedges and serve.

SLOW AND EASY BREAD IN A POT

I've never made any bread as simple or easy as this "potted" version. Even though it takes hours to proof (rise), I decided to include it here because it requires only minimal work and ordinary ingredients. Everything is combined in a nonstick pan and the dough is proofed and baked in the same pan, so there is little cleanup. I usually mix the dough at night, using tepid water, so the rising starts fairly quickly. The dough needs to rise for about an hour at room temperature and it develops during an overnight proofing in the refrigerator. In the morning, I remove the lid from the pan and bake the bread for an hour.

MAKES 1 TWO-POUND LOAF

2¼ cups tepid water (about 90 degrees)

1 teaspoon quick-rise yeast

1 tablespoon salt (or more to taste)

4 cups all-purpose flour (about 1 pound 5 ounces)

Combine the water, yeast, and salt in a nonstick saucepan (mine is 3.2 quarts) that is about 8 inches across and 4 inches deep. Add the flour and mix thoroughly with a sturdy wooden spoon for 30 seconds to 1 minute, or until the dough is well combined. Cover with a lid and let rise at room temperature (about 70 degrees) for 1 hour, until it bubbles and rises about 1 inch in the pot.

Even though the dough is only partially proofed, scrape the inside of the pot above the level of the dough with a rubber spatula to collect any soft pieces of dough clinging to the sides of the pot. Still using the rubber spatula, bring the edge of the dough in toward the center to deflate it. Cover and place in the refrigerator for 12 to 14 hours.

Preheat the oven to 425 degrees. Uncover the pan and bake for 1 hour, covering the bread loosely with a piece of aluminum foil after 45 minutes if it is getting too brown. Remove the bread from the oven and set aside for about 5 minutes to allow the bread to shrink from the sides of the pan. Unmold and cool on a wire rack for at least 1 hour before slicing.

DESSERTS

STILTON WITH APPLE, NUTS, AND PORT

We finish most of our meals at home with cheese rather than sweets. One of my favorite cheeses is blue cheese, particularly the hard Bleu de Gex from France, Gorgonzola from Italy, and Stilton from England. Fruit, nuts, and a glass of port wine are excellent matches with the cheese. A little lemon juice prevents the apple pieces from discoloring and a sprinkling of coarsely ground black pepper adds complexity. Port wine, the older the better, is a great complement and the perfect ending to a meal.

4 SERVINGS

About 24 pecan or walnut halves

1 large apple (8-10 ounces)

½ lemon

1 teaspoon coarsely ground black pepper

4 pieces Stilton cheese (about 4 ounces total)

4 glasses (about 4 ounces each) old port wine

Toasted bread rounds or crackers (optional)

Preheat the oven to 400 degrees. Spread the nuts on a baking sheet and roast them for about 6 minutes to intensify their flavor.

Quarter the apple and remove and discard the core. Cut each quarter into quarters (for 16 wedges total) and arrange 4 wedges on each of four dessert plates. Sprinkle with the lemon juice and coarse pepper. Add about 6 nuts to each plate, arranging them attractively between the apple wedges. Put a piece of cheese in the center of each plate. Serve with the port wine and, if you like, toasted bread or crackers.

BUTTER PECAN ICE CREAM WITH
APPLE MAPLE TOPPING

Caramelized apples are a perfect match for ice cream—try any of your favorite flavors, like vanilla, coffee, or butter pecan, a personal favorite of mine. Enhanced by maple syrup and butter, the apples can also be served on their own with a tablespoon of sour cream or mascarpone on top and a sprinkling of nuts. (Cookies are an optional addition.) Cortland, Russet, and McIntosh are a few of my favorite apples.

6 TO 8 SERVINGS

3 apples (about 1½ pounds total), Cortland or another variety to your liking

3 tablespoons unsalted butter

½ cup maple syrup

½ cup apple cider

1 quart good butter pecan ice cream, or another flavor you like

2 tablespoons crushed pistachio nuts

Peel and core the apples and cut them into 1-inch cubes. Put the cubes in a skillet, preferably nonstick, with the butter and maple syrup. Bring to a rolling boil, cover, reduce the heat to low, and cook gently for about 2 minutes. Uncover, increase the heat, and cook for about 5 minutes, until the liquid is gone and the mixture begins to sizzle. Continue cooking for 8 to 10 minutes longer, tossing the apples occasionally to keep them from burning. When you achieve a light caramel color, add the apple cider and bring to a boil. Transfer to a medium bowl and cool. The topping is best served at room temperature or slightly warm.

About 1 hour before serving, transfer the ice cream from the freezer to the refrigerator to soften. When ready to serve, place a scoop of ice cream on a dessert plate or in a bowl for each serving. Top with some of the apple mixture and a sprinkling of crushed pistachios.

SKILLET APPLE CHARLOTTE

A classic apple charlotte is made in a deep metal charlotte mold that has been lined with buttered bread slices and filled with sautéed caramelized apples and sometimes nuts. The apple mixture is then covered with more bread and the charlotte is baked, unmolded, and served with apricot sauce.

In this quick version, apple wedges are sautéed with honey and maple syrup, covered with buttered bread slices, baked and then turned out of the pan like a tart Tatin.

4 SERVINGS

3 Granny Smith apples (about 1½ pounds total)

3 tablespoons unsalted butter

2 tablespoons maple syrup

1 tablespoon honey

4 slices white bread

1 teaspoon sugar

3 tablespoons apricot preserves

About ½ cup sour cream or Greek yogurt (optional)

Preheat the oven to 400 degrees. Peel, core, and cut each apple into 6 wedges. Put the wedges in a small (7- to 8-inch) nonstick skillet and add 2 tablespoons of the butter, the maple syrup, and the honey. Bring to a boil over high heat. Cover, reduce the heat to low, and cook for about 5 minutes, or until the apples are just tender. Uncover and cook over high heat for 4 to 5 minutes, or until the liquid is completely gone, then continue cooking for another 2 minutes or so to glaze and caramelize the apples.

Trim the crusts from the bread slices and arrange them, touching, in a square on a cutting board. Trim the corners to create a rough disk that will fit into the skillet and cover the apples. Butter the bread on one side with the remaining 1 tablespoon butter and arrange the slices buttered side up on top of the apples. Sprinkle on the sugar and place the pan in the oven. Bake for about 15 minutes, or until the bread is nicely browned on top.

At serving time, if necessary, reheat the dessert on top of the stove to help loosen the apples and unmold the charlotte onto a serving platter. If the

apricot preserves are firm, heat them for 30 seconds in a microwave oven to soften. Pour and spread them on top of the apples. Serve the dessert in wedges as is or with a couple of tablespoons of sour cream or Greek yogurt, if you like.

SMALL BERRY CUSTARDS

Conventional berry tarts are made by baking a shell of cookie dough and, when it is cold, filling it with custard, arranging berries on top, and finishing it with a glaze. However, it is easier, faster, and less caloric to make this similar recipe without the dough. The custard is spooned into individual soufflé molds or small glass bowls and topped with berries glazed with seedless raspberry jam. Any small molds with about a ½-cup capacity that are pretty enough to serve in the dining room will work here.

4 SERVINGS

Pastry Cream

- 1¼ cups half-and-half
- ¼ teaspoon pure vanilla extract
- 2 large egg yolks
- 3 tablespoons sugar
- 2 tablespoons all-purpose flour

- 4 medium strawberries
- 1 small container (about 6 ounces) raspberries
- ¼ cup seedless raspberry jam
- 4 sprigs fresh mint, for garnish (optional)
- Store-bought cookies (optional)

For the pastry cream: Bring the half-and-half and vanilla to a boil in a small saucepan. Meanwhile, combine the egg yolks and sugar in a medium bowl with a whisk. Add the flour to the yolks and mix it in well with the whisk. Pour the hot half-and-half into the yolk mixture and whisk it in. Pour the entire mixture back into the saucepan and bring it to a boil, whisking until it thickens. Boil for 10 seconds longer, remove from the heat, and cool.

When ready to assemble the desserts, divide the cream among four ½-cup molds. Cut each strawberry lengthwise into 6 to 8 slices and stand the slices up all around the edge of the molds so the tips extend a little beyond the edge. Arrange a layer of raspberries on top of the cream in each mold inside the strawberry border. Heat the raspberry jam for about 10 seconds in a microwave if it is too firm to use as a glaze and coat the berries with the jam. Garnish with the mint sprigs if using. Serve with cookies, if you like.

PEAR COMPOTE WITH
ALMOND CRUMBLE COOKIES

Sweet and tart at the same time, this compote is the perfect fall concoction.
You can make the almond cookie dough in seconds in a food processor. The
cookies go well with almost any fruit dessert or with a cup of coffee or tea.

4 SERVINGS

1 pound pears, Bartlett,
Bosc, or another variety

1 large lime

1 cup apple cider

½ cup maple syrup

½ cup sour cream

Almond Crumble Cookies
(recipe follows)

Using a vegetable peeler or a sharp paring knife, peel
and core the pears. Cut them into 1-inch pieces and
put them in a large saucepan. Using a zester, cut
around the lime to remove thin strips of zest. Place
the lime in a microwave oven for 20 to 30 seconds.
This breaks the texture of the fruit and releases more
juice. Juice the lime. Add the zest and about 2 tablespoons of the lime juice to the saucepan containing
the pears. Stir in the cider and maple syrup and
bring to a boil. Cover and boil gently for 15 minutes, or until the pears are tender. Uncover and continue boiling for a few minutes longer, or until the
mixture thickens into a coarse puree.

Serve the compote cool or at room temperature,
garnished with zest and topped with a little sour
cream, accompanied by Almond Crumble Cookies.

ALMOND CRUMBLE COOKIES

ABOUT 2 DOZEN

1 cup whole unblanched almonds

½ cup all-purpose flour

2 tablespoons sugar

4 tablespoons (½ stick) cold unsalted butter

½ teaspoon pure vanilla extract

2 tablespoons water

½ cup confectioners' sugar

Preheat the oven to 350 degrees. Spread the almonds on a baking sheet and toast for about 8 minutes, or until lightly browned. Cool completely; leave the oven on. Line a cookie sheet with a reusable nonstick mat or spray it with nonstick cooking spray. Process the almonds, flour, and sugar in a food processor for about 30 seconds, or until powdery. Add the butter, vanilla, and water and process for 10 seconds, or until the dough comes together.

Divide the dough into about 24 pieces, each about the size of a large cherry. Roll the dough pieces between your palms to form balls and arrange the balls an inch or so apart on the lined cookie sheet. Using two fingers, flatten the cookies slightly. Bake for about 22 minutes, until lightly browned all over. Put the confectioners' sugar in a large bowl.

Let cool for a few minutes. While the cookies are still warm, toss or roll them in the confectioners' sugar to coat them on all sides. Transfer to a tray to cool completely. Store in an airtight container. They will keep for 2 weeks. Save any excess confectioners' sugar to use in other desserts.

PEARS BONNE FEMME

Apples bonne femme, or apples "good-lady" style, is a popular home recipe in France. The apples are baked for nearly an hour in the oven with butter, sugar, some jam, and lemon juice.

I use canned pears in my version, cooking them in some of the syrup with butter and apricot preserves for just a couple of minutes. Served at room temperature with a smidgen of whipped cream cheese on top, they are fast and delicious.

4 OR 5 SERVINGS

1 can (15 ounces) pear
  halves in syrup

2 tablespoons unsalted
  butter

2 tablespoons apricot
  preserves

4 tablespoons whipped
  cream cheese

  Cookies (optional)

Drain the pears, reserving the syrup. There should be about 5 pear halves and ¾ cup syrup. Pour ½ cup of the syrup into a large skillet with the butter, preserves, and pears and bring to a boil. Boil for 2 to 3 minutes, turning the pear halves in the syrup, until the mixture is thick and creamy. Transfer to a dish and cool to room temperature. Discard the remaining syrup.

Divide the pear halves among four or five dessert dishes, placing them cut side up. Place about 1 tablespoon whipped cream cheese in the cavity of each pear and spoon some sauce over them. Serve with cookies, if you like.

SECKEL PEARS IN COFFEE

This is the type of family recipe that combines thriftiness in the kitchen with a creative sense of cooking. It's ideal for when you have a pot of coffee left over from breakfast and an abundance of pears in your fruit bowl. The combination of reduced coffee, brown sugar, and vanilla creates a dark, rich sauce that is delicious with pears.

The cooking time depends entirely on the ripeness of the pears; I like to leave Seckel pears whole, but if these are unavailable, use about 1¼ pounds of a larger pear variety (like Bosc) and peel, quarter, and core them before cooking. Make sure to select pears of about the same ripeness; otherwise, some will fall apart before others cook through. This dessert can be made ahead and will keep, refrigerated, for several days. Serve with a slice of brioche or pound cake.

4 SERVINGS

About ¼ cup sliced almonds

4 large Seckel pears (about 1¼ pounds total), peeled, seeded and cored with a melon baller

2 cups brewed coffee

¼ cup light brown sugar

½ teaspoon pure vanilla extract

1 teaspoon potato starch (available in the kosher section of most supermarkets)

1 tablespoon water

¼ cup cream sherry, Madeira, or port wine

4 slices brioche or pound cake

1-2 tablespoons cocoa nibs or good chocolate grated with a vegetable peeler, for garnish

4 sprigs fresh mint

COCOA NIBS

Cocoa nibs are the dark, crunchy roasted cocoa bean nuggets that have been removed from their husks. Intensely flavored and unsweetened, they are the pure essence of cacao and the basic ingredient for chocolate. They are found in specialty shops and can be used as an ingredient in both sweet and savory dishes. They are available from Scharffen Berger Chocolate Maker online at www.scharffenberger.com.

Preheat the oven to 400 degrees. Spread the sliced almonds on a baking sheet and toast for 6 to 8 minutes, until lightly browned. Set aside.

Put the pears, coffee, brown sugar, and vanilla in a medium saucepan and bring to a boil. Boil gently, covered, until the pears are tender, 10 to 12 minutes. Transfer the pears to a bowl. Boil the syrup to reduce it, if necessary, to about ¾ cup. Dissolve the potato starch in the water, add to the syrup, and return to a boil. Pour over the pears, add the sherry, and mix well. Cover and cool.

To serve, put a slice of brioche or pound cake in each of four dessert bowls, preferably glass. Sit a pear on top, coat with the syrup, and garnish with the almonds, cocoa nibs or grated chocolate, and mint.

CRISP PEAR TART

Using a 7-inch flour tortilla as the "crust" or shell and Bartlett or Anjou pears that are ripe enough to eat as the fruit topping, you can make a fast and easy fruit tart. To make certain that the crust is crisp and caramelized on the bottom, butter and sugar the underside of the tortilla before topping it with the pears. Some of the mixture usually runs out from the bottom of the tart and the tart may burn lightly around the edge, but I don't mind a dark, caramelized edge on my tart shell. If you object to it, you can trim a little of it off.

4 SERVINGS

1 (7-inch) flour tortilla

2 tablespoons unsalted butter, softened

3 tablespoons sugar

2 medium firm but ripe Bartlett or Anjou pears (about ¾ pound total)

3 tablespoons apricot preserves

1 tablespoon pistachio nuts

Preheat the oven to 400 degrees. Place the tortilla in the center of a cookie sheet lined with a reusable nonstick mat. Spread 1 tablespoon of the butter on top of the tortilla and sprinkle it with 1 tablespoon of the sugar. Turn the tortilla over so the buttered side is underneath.

Peel, core, and cut each pear into about 12 wedges. Beginning at the edge of the tortilla, start arranging the wedges in a concentric circle with the thin edge of each wedge facing toward the center of the tortilla. Create another slightly overlapping circle, working in toward the center of the tortilla. Add additional rows with the remaining wedges, ending with a few pear pieces in the center to complete what will look like a large rose. Scatter the remaining 1 tablespoon butter, divided into pieces, on top and sprinkle with the remaining 2 tablespoons sugar.

Bake for 30 minutes, or until the pear slices are tender and the tortilla is crisp and browned. Remove from the oven, set aside for a minute or so, then lift the tart with a spatula and transfer it to a rack to cool, discarding any burned bits around it.

Heat the apricot preserves, if too thick to use as a glaze, in a microwave oven for about 10 seconds to liquefy. Spread the glaze on top of the tart. Cut the tart into 4 wedges, sprinkle with pistachios, and serve at room temperature.

PEACH MELBA

The original version of this dessert was created for the Australian soprano Nellie Melba by Auguste Escoffier, the famous French chef who lived from 1846 to 1935. Consisting of poached peaches, raspberry coulis, and ice cream, it is simple to make with canned peaches. I especially like the large yellow cling peach halves in heavy syrup.

4 SERVINGS

2 tablespoons sliced almonds

1 cup frozen raspberries (Individually Quick Frozen, or IQF), defrosted

3 tablespoons seedless raspberry preserves

1 can (15.25 ounces) peach halves

1 pint good vanilla ice cream

4 sprigs fresh mint, for garnish (optional)

Preheat the oven to 400 degrees. Spread the almonds on a baking sheet and toast in the oven for 6 to 8 minutes, or until lightly browned. Set aside.

Push the raspberries and preserves through a food mill. If some of the seeds from the berries go through the screen, you can strain them again through a sieve, if you like. You should have about ½ cup raspberry sauce.

Drain the peaches. You should have 4 halves. Place a ½-cup scoop vanilla ice cream in each of four dessert dishes or stemmed glasses. Top with a peach half, rounded side up. Coat the peach in each glass with some of the raspberry sauce and sprinkle the almonds on top. Garnish with mint, if you like, and serve.

SWEET RICOTTA GÂTEAUX WITH PEACH SAUCE

The ricotta cream in this super-simple dessert is similar to the filling for Italian cannoli: ricotta cheese (get the best quality), sugar, and vanilla mixed together until fluffy. The filling is sandwiched between graham crackers and some diluted peach or apricot jam is spooned over. Graham crackers usually come in 5-by-2½-inch rectangles. Use a serrated knife to cut each cracker into two squares. If assembled just before serving, the crackers will be quite crisp; stuffed ahead, they will soften somewhat. Either way, the dessert is good.

4 SERVINGS

⅔ cup best-quality ricotta cheese

¼ teaspoon pure vanilla extract

1 tablespoon sugar

4 graham crackers, each cut into two 2½-inch squares

6 tablespoons peach or apricot jam with pieces of fruit in it, preferably homemade

About 1 tablespoon cognac, rum, or water

About 12 hazelnuts, whole or broken into pieces

Using a whisk or spoon, stir the ricotta, vanilla, and sugar in a small bowl until smooth and fluffy. Spread 4 of the graham cracker squares with the ricotta cream and place them in the center of four dessert plates. Top with the 4 remaining squares.

Mix the jam with enough cognac, rum, or water to thin it enough to coat the crackers. Spoon about 1½ tablespoons of the diluted jam over each dessert, top with the hazelnuts, and serve.

APRICOT CLAFOUTIS

A clafoutis is somewhere between a sweet omelet and a custard. Made with fruit, often cherries or apples, it is a classic throughout France, with small variations from region to region and, sometimes, different names. It can be called *flan aux fruits* or a *flognarde,* but most often is known as clafoutis.

My recipe is made with canned apricots. Try different brands: some are much better than others. Serve the clafoutis directly from the skillet or unmold it onto a serving plate and serve in wedges.

4 SERVINGS

3 tablespoons unsalted butter

1 can (8.25 ounces) apricot halves in syrup

¼ cup all-purpose flour

3 large eggs

2 tablespoons sugar

¼ cup sour cream

1 tablespoon confectioners' sugar

Preheat the oven to 400 degrees. Melt the butter in an 8-inch nonstick skillet.

Drain the apricots, reserving the syrup. You should have 6 to 8 apricot halves and ½ cup syrup. Using a whisk, mix the syrup with the flour in a medium bowl. Add the eggs, sugar, sour cream, and 1 tablespoon of the melted butter from the skillet and mix until you have a smooth batter.

Pour the batter into the butter remaining in the skillet and arrange the apricot halves on top, spacing them evenly. Place the skillet over high heat for about 2 minutes and then transfer it to the oven. Bake for 18 to 20 minutes, or until lightly browned and puffy. Remove from the oven and sprinkle the confectioners' sugar on top. Cool to lukewarm.

Serve the clafoutis directly from the skillet in wedges or unmold. To unmold, make certain that the clafoutis is free from the sides of the pan; if necessary, run a sharp knife around the edge to release it. Then place a piece of plastic wrap on top of the dessert and invert it onto a plate. Place another plate on top of the inverted clafoutis and invert it again so the crusty side is on top. Remove the plastic wrap, cut into wedges, and serve.

CRISP APRICOT GALETTE

This dessert is ideal for last-minute guests: all you need is a flour tortilla, a can of apricot halves, and a few nuts. Be sure to line your cookie sheet with a non-stick mat, because the caramelized bottom of the galette would stick to the metal sheet.

4 SERVINGS

1 (7-inch) flour tortilla

1½ tablespoons unsalted butter, softened

1½ tablespoons sugar

1 can (15 ounces) apricot halves in syrup

1 tablespoon crushed hazelnuts

Preheat the oven to 400 degrees. Line a cookie sheet with a nonstick mat. Place the tortilla in the center of the cookie sheet. Spread about half the butter on the tortilla. Sprinkle about 1 tablespoon of the sugar on top. Turn the tortilla over so the buttered and sugared side is underneath.

Drain the can of apricots, reserving ½ cup of the syrup. You should have 10 to 12 apricot halves. Starting at the outer edge of the tortilla, arrange the apricot halves hollow side up in a single layer on the tortilla and place a tiny piece of butter from the remaining ¾ tablespoon in the hollow of each apricot half. Sprinkle the remaining ½ tablespoon sugar on the apricots and around the edge of the tortilla.

Bake for 25 minutes; the tortilla should be very crisp. Don't worry if some of the juice from the apricots has run onto the mat and burned. About 1 minute after the galette has been removed from the oven, transfer it with a large spatula to a wire rack to cool.

Pour the reserved syrup from the apricots into a small skillet and bring to a boil. Boil for 3 to 4 minutes, or until the syrup is reduced to about 3 tablespoons. Sprinkle the hazelnuts over the galette and spoon the syrup over the apricots to glaze them on top. Cut into wedges and serve at room temperature.

SAUTÉED STUFFED FIGS WITH BLUEBERRIES

I like dried figs and use them liberally in stews and enjoy them as snacks. In Portugal, figs are dried, split open, stuffed with almonds, and hung in the open markets, where they are sold. I stuff the opened figs with walnut halves and cook them in butter, honey, and white wine in a skillet to create a sauce, then sprinkle them with blueberries. Choose soft, moist figs that are as large as possible. The blueberries add color and texture to the dish, but you can omit them or substitute raisins or pomegranate seeds.

4 SERVINGS

12 dried figs (7-8 ounces total)

12 walnut halves

2 tablespoons unsalted butter

½ cup dry fruity white wine

⅓ cup honey

1 cup blueberries

Cut the figs into halves and arrange them flesh side up on a platter. Press 1 walnut half into each fig half and press on the nut to embed it well.

Melt the butter in a medium nonstick saucepan and add the wine and honey. Arrange the figs, walnut side up, in the pan and bring to a boil. Cover and boil gently for about 2 minutes, or until the mixture is syrupy and the figs are glazed.

Let the figs cool to room temperature. Arrange them, walnut side up, on a platter. Pour the sauce over the figs and sprinkle the blueberries on top. Serve.

PINEAPPLE IN DARK RUM SAUCE

The success of this dessert depends entirely on the ripeness of the pineapple. It should be yellow at the base and have a wonderful aroma. Only about half a pineapple is needed for this dessert; enjoy the other half plain the following day.

4 SERVINGS

1 ripe pineapple (about 3 pounds)

1 lime

3 tablespoons dark rum

½ cup honey

4 tablespoons mascarpone cheese

Cookies (optional)

Peel the pineapple and remove and discard the leaves, eyes, and any dark spots. Cut in half lengthwise and remove the core. Reserve half the pineapple for another use. Place the other half cut side down on a cutting board and, using a sharp knife, cut it into very thin (⅛-inch-thick) slices. Alternatively, if you are not proficient with a knife, use a Japanese vegetable slicer. You should have about 24 slices, or 6 per person. Arrange the slices, overlapping them slightly, in a large bowl or gratin dish.

Using a Microplane or ordinary grater, grate the zest of the lime and set it aside. Press on the lime to help release the juices, then halve and squeeze it to get 2 tablespoons juice. Combine the lime juice with the rum and honey in a small bowl and mix well. Pour the mixture over the pineapple, cover, and refrigerate until you are ready to serve.

At serving time, arrange 6 slices of pineapple on each of four plates, working from the outside of the plate to the center and positioning the slices so they resemble the petals of a flower. Pour the sauce over the pineapple and spoon a tablespoon of mascarpone into the center holes. Sprinkle with the grated lime zest and serve with cookies, if you like.

MANGO WITH NUTELLA SAUCE

Nutella, a hazelnut spread with chocolate that is available in jars in most supermarkets, combined with melted ice cream, creates a smooth, unctuous dessert sauce. The sauce is ideal to serve as a substitute for a custard cream when you have to produce a dessert at the last moment. This dessert can be prepared with different fruits, anything from bananas to pineapple to raspberries. Choose the ripest fruit, which will have the most flavor.

4 SERVINGS

1 cup good vanilla ice cream

⅓ cup Nutella

4 small slices (½ inch thick) pound cake

2 ripe mangoes (about ¾ pound each)

Lavender flowers, for garnish (optional)

Let the ice cream melt at room temperature in a medium bowl. Heat the Nutella in a microwave oven for a minute or so to soften it and then add it to the melted ice cream. Mix well with a whisk and set aside.

Trim the slices of pound cake, removing the dark edges, and cut into sticks about 3 inches long.

Using a sharp, thin-bladed knife, halve the mangoes lengthwise, cutting as close as possible to either side of the large, central pit. Using a large spoon, scoop out the flesh from each half mango in one piece. (As a bonus, the cook can eat the remaining flesh around the pits.)

At serving time, divide the sauce among four dessert plates and place a mango half in the middle of each plate. Arrange the pound cake sticks around the mango, garnish with lavender flowers, if you like, and serve.

TAPIOCA BANANA COCONUT PUDDING

Tapioca is the perfect comfort dessert—simple, homey, soft, creamy, and smooth—just what the doctor ordered when you feel a bit queasy or need to be soothed or cheered up.

Made with Minute tapioca, this pudding cooks in a flash. For an extra-rich, exotic note, I cook the tapioca in coconut milk and regular milk, although the tapioca can be made with just regular milk. Honey gives the dessert sweetness, lime zest lends freshness, and dried cranberries add texture, tang, and color.

Coconut milk comes in cans; the milk is sometimes solid in the top half of the can, with the liquid underneath. Mix the contents of the can together until well blended before using.

4 SERVINGS

1 cup canned coconut milk

1 cup whole milk, plus a few more tablespoons if needed

½ cup Minute tapioca

⅓ cup honey

2 teaspoons grated lime zest

⅓ cup dried cranberries

2 bananas

Combine the coconut milk and milk in a medium saucepan and sprinkle the tapioca on top. Mix the tapioca in with a whisk and bring to a boil, stirring occasionally. Reduce the heat and boil gently for 1 minute. Remove from the heat and stir in the honey, lime zest, and cranberries. The pudding should be creamy and soft. If it is too thick, add a couple of additional tablespoons milk.

When the pudding is at room temperature, peel and slice the bananas into the pudding. Mix well. (The banana slices will not discolor if covered well with the pudding.) Refrigerate until cold. Serve in deep dishes or glasses.

CREAM CHEESE AND FRUIT MEDLEY

This combination of fruit, honey, and soft cheese is elegant, rich, and concentrated. The portions should be small: an 8-ounce container of whipped cream cheese is more than enough for four servings.

There are many dried fruits to choose from at the supermarket—from dried papaya to dried blueberries—and they make great snacks and desserts as well as good additions to stuffings. Although the cream cheese and fruit can be served simply, with a few tablespoons of the cream cheese and fruit mixture spooned onto plates and additional fruit arranged on top, the dessert is fancier when shaped in a mold. Any small can (about 1¾ inches in diameter) with the ends removed will work.

4 SERVINGS

1 cup diced (½-inch) dried fruits (apricots, strawberries, blueberries, cranberries, cherries, figs, papayas, apples, and/or dates)

2 tablespoons fresh lime juice (grate zest first or remove strips of zest)

¼ cup honey

1 tablespoon water

1 container (8 ounces) whipped cream cheese

A few cookies, crumbled

1 teaspoon grated lime zest or zest strips

Combine the dried fruit in a bowl with the lime juice, honey, and water. This can be done a few hours ahead, if you like.

Place a mold (see headnote) in the center of a dessert plate. Spoon about 1½ tablespoons cream cheese into the bottom of the mold and press on it gently to make a smooth, even layer. Add about ⅓ cup of the fruit mixture to the mold, then add a layer of crumbled cookies, and press another 1½ tablespoons cream cheese on top, enclosing the fruit between the 2 cream cheese layers. Push gently on the contents of the mold with the back of a spoon and slide off the mold. The desserts will hold the shape of the mold. Repeat this procedure on the three remaining plates.

Sprinkle the remaining fruit, juice, and zest around and over the top of the desserts. Serve.

Grapefruit Suprêmes

Especially around the Christmas holidays, I often make candied orange, lemon, or grapefruit peels to give to friends. Sometimes I partially dip the candied orange peels, called *orangette,* into melted chocolate to serve as an after-dinner treat. When I candy grapefruit peel, I prefer pink or ruby red grapefruit, which has beautifully colored, flavorful skin that becomes transparent when cooked. I don't object to the slightly bitter taste that always remains in the candied grapefruit skin, but if you do, make the recipe with orange peel.

For this recipe, I cut the skin, including the white pith underneath, into sticks and cook them in sugar syrup until they are crystallized. After removing the segments of grapefruit flesh from between the membranes, I serve them with a few dried cranberries and the grapefruit juice sweetened with the syrup used to cook the peel. The crowning touch is the addition of the candied grapefruit peel.

4 SERVINGS

2 pink or ruby red grapefruits (about 1 pound each)

⅓ cup plus ½ cup sugar

¼ cup dried cranberries, dried cherries, or raisins

2 tablespoons Grand Marnier

4 sprigs fresh mint, for garnish (optional)

Cut off the top and bottom of the grapefruits, so the flesh is exposed. Place the grapefruits flesh side down on the table and cut off all the skin and pith with a sharp knife. Trim off the rough ends of the peel and cut it into sticks about ⅜ inch wide and 2½ inches long. Cut about 20 sticks; one grapefruit skin will be more than enough.

Transfer the peel to a small saucepan, cover with about 3 cups water, and bring to a boil. Boil for 1 minute and then drain in a colander. Rinse the peel under cold tap water and wash the saucepan to remove any bitter residue. Repeat this blanching process once more to remove additional bitterness. Drain and rinse the peel and wash the saucepan well again.

Put the peel sticks back in the saucepan with ¾ cup water and ⅓ cup of the sugar. Bring to a boil and boil over medium heat for about 15 minutes, or until the mixtures thickens and becomes bubbly and sticky. The peels should be transparent. Let rest for 1 minute.

Meanwhile, spread the remaining ½ cup sugar on a sheet of aluminum foil. Using a fork, lift the peels from the pan (reserving the 1 to 2 tablespoons syrup in the pan) and drop them into the sugar. Separate the peels with the fork and your fingers and roll and press them into the sugar to coat them well all over. Arrange the candied peels on a platter to cool. They will become hard on the surface but remain moist inside. When cool, transfer to a plastic container with a tight-fitting lid and refrigerate. (The candied peels will keep for several weeks, refrigerated in a covered container.)

Using a paring knife, cut the segments of flesh from between the membranes of the grapefruit. You should have about 12 segments from each grapefruit. Holding the membranes over a bowl, squeeze them to extract the juice. To sweeten the juice, add ½ cup of it to the reserved syrup in the pan.

At serving time, arrange 6 segments of grapefruit on each of four dessert plates. Sprinkle 8 to 10 dried cranberries, cherries, or raisins on top of each serving and drizzle the syrup in the pan over the top. Sprinkle on a little Grand Marnier. Garnish with mint, if using. Serve with some of the candied peels, arranged around the desserts or on a separate plate.

CHERRIES IN ARMAGNAC SAUCE WITH POUND CAKE

I always have a couple of cans of cherries in my pantry, usually the large Bing cherries from Oregon or Washington State and, often, tart cherries. These are handy for a fast dessert and are great with ice cream. I reduce the cherry juice from the can, thicken it lightly, and add a little Armagnac or cognac at the end. If you object to the alcohol, you can omit it. Served over store-bought pound cake with a dollop of sour cream on top, this dessert is delicious warm or cold.

4 SERVINGS

1 **can (about 15 ounces) pitted Bing or tart cherries**

½ **teaspoon potato starch (available in the kosher section of most supermarkets)**

1 **tablespoon water**

2 **tablespoons Armagnac or cognac**

4 **slices (about ½ inch thick) store-bought pound cake**

¼ **cup sour cream**

4 **sprigs fresh mint, for garnish**

Drain the can of cherries, reserving the juice. You should have about ¾ cup juice and 1½ cups cherries. Pour the juice into a small skillet and boil until it is reduced to about ½ cup, about 2 minutes.

Combine the potato starch with the water in a small bowl and add it to the reduced juice, stirring it in well to thicken the juice. Add the cherries and the Armagnac or cognac and bring to a boil.

Place a slice of pound cake on each of four plates. Divide the warm cherries among the plates, spooning them over and around the cake. Pour the juice over the cherries and cake, top with a dollop of sour cream, garnish with the mint, and serve.

GREEK YOGURT, WALNUTS, AND HONEY

A simple mixture of yogurt and honey is served for dessert in small restaurants all over the Greek Islands. The yogurt is so luscious, smooth, and rich that it rivals our sour cream and the honey is usually thick, dark, pungent, and flavorful. Fortunately, Greek yogurt is widely available in this country. Walnuts, a staple of Greek cuisine, as well as mint, find their way into my interpretation of this dish. About ½ cup of yogurt per person is sufficient and the addition of sour cream makes it closer in flavor and texture to the kind I enjoyed in Greece.

4 SERVINGS

About 2 cups Greek yogurt

About ⅓ cup sour cream

8 walnut halves, each broken in half

8 tablespoons of the best honey available

1 tablespoon shredded fresh peppermint or spearmint leaves

1 tablespoon grated lemon zest

Mix the yogurt and sour cream together in a bowl and divide among four dessert plates. Sprinkle the walnuts on top and drizzle about 2 tablespoons honey over the yogurt mixture on each plate. Top with the mint and lemon zest. Serve.

MINI ALMOND CAKES IN RASPBERRY SAUCE

These mini almond cakes are quite easy to make, but if you are pressed for time, substitute rounds of store-bought pound cake.

The recipe also can be made into one larger cake and both the large cake and the mini cakes can be made ahead and frozen. I cook my little cakes in the small aluminum-foil muffin cups that come with paper liners. Soak the cakes in the raspberry sauce for an hour or so before serving if you like them really saturated.

4 SERVINGS

¼ cup whole unblanched almonds

¼ cup sugar

¼ cup all-purpose flour

¼ teaspoon baking powder

1 large egg

3 tablespoons unsalted butter, melted

2 tablespoons dark rum

1½ cups frozen raspberries (Individually Quick Frozen, or IQF), defrosted

⅓ cup strawberry preserves

½ cup blueberries

½ cup sliced or diced (½-inch) strawberries

4 sprigs fresh mint, for garnish

Preheat the oven to 350 degrees. Line the bottoms of 4 aluminum-foil muffin cups with the paper liners included in the package. Arrange the lined cups on a baking sheet. Put the almonds, sugar, flour, and baking powder in a small food processor and process until smooth. In a medium bowl, whisk together the egg, melted butter, and rum until well combined. Add the almond mixture and whisk again lightly until combined. Divide the batter among the cups. Bake for 15 minutes, or until puffy and browned. Unmold and cool on a rack.

Meanwhile, push the defrosted raspberries and preserves through a food mill. If there are fine seeds in the sauce and you object to them, strain the mixture through a sieve. You should have about 1 cup sauce.

Remove and discard the liners from the cakes. Roll them in the raspberry sauce to coat them on all sides. Place a cake in the center of each of four dessert plates, spoon some sauce on top of and around the cakes, and add a sprinkling of blueberries and strawberry pieces and a sprig of mint to each. Serve.

COOKIE DOUGH RASPBERRY TART

Packaged cookie dough from the supermarket for the crust makes this beautiful tart very easy. Although I use sugar cookie dough, the tart can also be prepared with chocolate chip cookie dough, since raspberries and chocolate are perfect partners. Raspberries, often a bit tart, help cut down on the dough's sweetness. I glaze the top of the tart with seedless raspberry jam that I microwave just long enough to warm and thin it slightly, so it can be poured over the berries.

4 SERVINGS

6 ounces sugar cookie dough, or any other ready-made cookie dough you like

1 pint fresh raspberries

½ cup seedless raspberry jam

½ cup sour cream

Pomegranate seeds or sprig fresh mint for garnish (optional)

Preheat the oven to 375 degrees. Line a cookie sheet with a reusable nonstick mat or with parchment paper. Place the cookie dough between two pieces of plastic wrap and press down on it with your hands or a rolling pin to extend it to an 8-inch circle. Don't worry if it is not exactly round. Remove the plastic sheet from the top and invert the dough onto the lined baking sheet. With your fingers, fold the outside edge of the dough back on itself a little to make it thicker at the periphery and the circle as round as possible. Press and pinch the dough lightly at the edge to create an attractive border. If the dough gets too soft and sticky to mold, return it to the refrigerator for 10 to 15 minutes to firm up before continuing.

Bake for 9 to 10 minutes, or until nicely browned and crisp. The dough circle will expand to about 9 inches. Let rest to cool and harden for 15 minutes before transferring to a serving platter.

At serving time, or no more than 30 minutes before serving, arrange the berries in one layer on the tart shell. Heat the jam to lukewarm to thin it a little and spoon it over the berries to coat them. (If this is done too far ahead, the shell will soften because of the moisture in the berries and jam.) Cut the tart into 4 wedges with a serrated knife and serve with dollops of sour cream and a sprinkling of pomegranate seeds or mint, if desired.

CHOCOLATE ROCHERS WITH HAZELNUTS AND CORNFLAKES

For lovers of chocolate like me, this is an ideal recipe for the holidays. *Rochers* is a French word meaning rocks, or little boulders, which is what these little chocolate confections look like. My friend, the chocolate king Jacques Torres, makes something similar, which gave me this idea. Here, some of the *rochers* are studded with cornflakes and some with hazelnuts, but Rice Krispies, dried cherries, granola, or any other dried fruit or cereal can be used in the same manner. The *rochers* can be smaller or larger, based on your own tastes, and you can make them with semisweet chocolate morsels or milk chocolate or bittersweet chocolate. I like bittersweet best because it is high in cocoa content and not too sweet.

35 TO 55, DEPENDING ON SIZE

12 ounces bittersweet chocolate

1½ cups whole hazelnuts or almonds

2½ cups cornflakes or Rice Krispies

Break the chocolate into 1-inch pieces and put them in a glass bowl. Microwave on high for about 1½ minutes. At this point, the chocolate may look like it has not started to melt. Wait 4 to 5 minutes and microwave the chocolate again for 1 minute. (Waiting helps prevent the chocolate from scorching or burning.) Stir after the second minute in the microwave; the chocolate should be almost melted. Wait a few more minutes and microwave the chocolate again for 30 seconds. Stir with a rubber spatula. The chocolate should be glossy and smooth. (You should have about 1 cup melted chocolate.)

For hazelnut *rochers*: Preheat the oven to 350 degrees. Scatter the hazelnuts or almonds on a cookie sheet and toast for 7 to 8 minutes. Do not worry about the skin. Transfer the nuts to a medium bowl and pour about ½ cup of the melted chocolate on top. Mix well with a spoon to coat the nuts with the chocolate. Line a cookie sheet with plastic wrap.

Using a tablespoon, scoop up a spoonful of the chocolate-hazelnut mixture and push the dough off the tablespoon with a teaspoon onto the lined cookie sheet. Repeat, making 15 to 25 rochers, depending on size. Cool until hardened. (Stored in an airtight container, the *rochers* will keep for 2 to 3 weeks in the refrigerator or up to 2 months in the freezer.)

For cornflake *rochers*: Put the cornflakes in a medium bowl and add the remaining ½ cup melted chocolate. Mix well with a spoon until combined. Do not worry if the cornflakes break somewhat; keep mixing until they are coated. Spoon the small mounds onto the lined cookie sheet. You will have 20 to 30, depending on size. Cool until hardened. (These can also be frozen.)

CHESTNUT CREAM MONT BLANC

Mont Blanc, or white mountain dessert, is made with meringue that is covered with a sweet chestnut puree and topped with whipped cream decorated with crystallized violets. I remember how many hours it took me to peel, cook, and puree the chestnuts with vanilla and sugar when I was an apprentice in France. Meringues are also time-consuming to make. Sweet canned chestnut puree, also called chestnut spread, is available at many supermarkets or at specialty stores, and it is great to have a couple of jars on hand for this fast dessert.

I have not found commercially made meringues to be very good, but I can get great individually wrapped biscotti at my market. I use chocolate biscotti in this dessert because chocolate goes so well with the chestnut spread, which I flavor with dark rum. The only work required is to whip ½ cup of cream, which takes only about 2 minutes, but if you don't have the time for it, use a tablespoon of mascarpone or crème fraîche on each serving instead. I can usually find crystallized violets or roses in specialty stores, but a sprig of mint can be substituted as a decoration.

4 SERVINGS

1 can (8.75 ounces) sweetened chestnut spread

2 tablespoons dark rum (optional)

4 chocolate biscotti (about ¾ ounce each)

½ cup heavy cream

4 crystallized violets, for decoration (optional), or 4 fresh sprigs mint

Mix the chestnut spread with the rum, if using. Break the biscotti into pieces. (If they are individually wrapped, crack them while still in their wrappers with the base of a small pan.) Arrange the biscotti pieces in four martini glasses or other nice glasses.

Spoon the chestnut spread over the biscotti in each glass. Whip the cream until firm and add a few spoonfuls of whipped cream to each dessert. Top with the crystallized violets or mint and serve.

JAM TARTINES WITH FRUIT SHERBET

A *tartine* is a thin slice of bread spread with butter, jam, or any other spread. Children in France often enjoy this impromptu treat at the *quatre heure,* the French name for an after-school snack. I often make a simple sweet with pound cake and jam and serve it with sherbet and, when I have them, fresh berries.

4 SERVINGS

About ⅓ cup seedless raspberry preserves

About ⅓ cup apricot jam

4 slices (½ inch thick) best-quality pound cake

1 pint strawberry, orange, or mango sherbet

½ cup blueberries, raspberries, or blackberries (optional)

Soften the raspberry preserves and the apricot jam for about 30 seconds in a microwave oven. Spread the softened raspberry preserves on two of the pound cake slices and the softened apricot jam on the other two slices. Trim the edges of the slices, then cut each into rectangles, triangles, or squares. Arrange a few jam *tartines* on each of four dessert plates and place a scoop of sherbet in the center. Sprinkle on a few berries, if desired, and serve.

POPOVER WITH APRICOT JAM

Popovers are a great last-minute dessert that "pop up" in the oven. This one has a creamy consistency inside, somewhat like a pancake. I serve it with apricot jam.

In summer I make fresh apricot jam by mixing very ripe apricot pieces with sugar in a roasting pan and baking the mixture, uncovered, in a 180-degree oven for up to 24 hours. I do the same with strawberries and peaches, but I think the apricot jam goes best with this popover.

4 SERVINGS

4 tablespoons (½ stick) unsalted butter

½ cup all-purpose flour

¼ cup sour cream

2 large eggs

2 tablespoons sugar

¼ teaspoon salt

½ cup milk

¼ cup apricot jam or preserves

About 1 tablespoon confectioners' sugar, for garnish

Preheat the oven to 425 degrees. Melt the butter in an 8-inch nonstick ovenproof skillet. In a medium bowl, mix the flour, sour cream, and eggs with a whisk until smooth. Add the sugar, salt, and milk and mix well. Pour about 3 tablespoons of the melted butter from the skillet into the batter and mix until it is incorporated.

Pour the batter into the remaining butter in the skillet and bake for 20 minutes. The batter should puff up the sides of the pan and brown nicely all over.

Remove from the oven and let the popover sit for a few minutes in the pan. Slide it onto a platter and spread the center with the apricot jam. Sprinkle confectioners' sugar around the edges, cut into 4 wedges, and serve.

The Menus

Small Crocks of Shrimp in Hot Vegetable Broth (74)
Pork Medallions with Grapes in Pomegranate Sauce (110)
Spinach, Macadamia Nuts, and Raisins (135)
Butter Pecan Ice Cream with Apple Maple Topping (173)

Cream of Leek and Mushroom Soup (36)
Stuffed Pork Tenderloin on Grape Tomatoes (113)
Mini Almond Cakes in Raspberry Sauce (208)

Criques (Potato Pancakes) on Mesclun Salad (144)
Chili con Carne with Lettuce and Cheese (106)
Crunchy Kale (128)
Pears Bonne Femme (181)

Shrimp with Cabbage and Red Caviar (68)
Ratatouille with Penne (155)
Peach Melba (186)

Lobster Roll Medallions on Spinach Salad (73)
Quick Lamb Stew (115)
Small Berry Custards (177)

Tomato Surprise (56)
Grilled Striped Bass with Romesco Sauce (78)
Pumpkin Gratin (138)
Cherries in Armagnac Sauce with Pound Cake (204)

Bold and Spicy Gazpacho (26)
Shellfish and Chicken Paella (89)
Pineapple in Dark Rum Sauce (195)

Rigatoni with Lettuce and Eggplant (160)
Steamed Fish and Shellfish Baskets (86)
Sautéed Julienned Endive (125)
Sautéed Stuffed Figs with Blueberries (194)

Seafood Chowder (32)
Crusty Chicken Thighs with Mushroom Sauce (97)
Fricassee of Brussels Sprouts and Bacon (132)
Stilton with Apple, Nuts, and Port (172)

Gnocchi with Eggs and Scallions (44)
Skirt Steak Grandma (104)
Sautéed Curly Mustard Greens with Hot Sausage (126)
Chestnut Cream Mont Blanc (214)

Hearty Vegetable Bean Soup (29)
Chicken Suprêmes with Tapenade and Mushroom Sauce (94)
Vegetable Couscous (154)
Pear Compote with Almond Crumble Cookies (178)

Smoked Salmon Pizza (164)
Roasted Split Chicken with Mustard Crust (99)
Fluffy Mashed Potatoes (142)
Greek Yogurt, Walnuts, and Honey (207)

Butternut Squash Velvet (35) or Sweet Potato Soup (30)
Fillet of Sole with Mushroom Sauce (85)
Peas, Mushrooms, and Endive (131)
Seckel Pears in Coffee (182)

Bluefin Tuna Tartare with Apple (70)
Lamb Burgers with Feta Cheese and Yogurt-Cucumber Sauce (120)
Corn Parfait (139)
Cream Cheese and Fruit Medley (199)

Picante Mussel Pilaf (64)
Onion-Crusted Sole with Anchovy Butter (80)
Apricot Clafoutis (190)

Bay Scallops in Mignonnette Sauce (67)
Sausage Patties with Pumpkin Seeds and Mushrooms (109)
Cornmeal Mush (151)
Crisp Pear Tart (184)

Asparagus Fans with Mustard Sauce (49)
Scallops Grenobloise (77)
Potato Gratin with Cream (143)
Jam Tartines with Fruit Sherbet (215)

Mini Savory Cheesecakes on Arugula or Butterhead Lettuce (42)
Steamed Scrod Packages in Pimiento Sauce (79)
Butternut Squash Sauté (136)
Tapioca Banana Coconut Pudding (197)

Risotto with Broccoli Stems (148)
Salmon Burgers on Baby Arugula (84)
Tibetan Flatbread (167)
Grapefruit Suprêmes (200)

Tall Greek Tomato Salad (52)
Poached Salmon in Sour Cream–Herb Sauce (83)
Stew of Peas and Carrots (129)
Sweet Ricotta Gâteaux with Peach Sauce (189)

Scallop Pancakes on Boston Lettuce Salad (61)
Lamb Curry (118)
Rice with Raisins (147)
Crisp Apricot Galette (193)

Chorizo, Mushroom, and Cheese Pizza (163)
Orecchiette with Fennel and Tuna (162)
Popover with Apricot Jam (217)

Frisée aux Lardons (Curly Endive with Bacon Bits) (53)
Spaghetti with Fresh Tomato and Anchovy Sauce (159)
Chocolate Rochers with Hazelnuts and Cornflakes (212)

Cocotte Eggs with Creamed Mushrooms (40)
Ragout of Broccolini, Beans, and Sausage (134)
Slow and Easy Bread in a Pot (168)
Cookie Dough Raspberry Tart (210)

Baked Clams Madison (62)
Cod in Olive-Tomato Crust (82)
Skillet Broccoli Bits (124)
Mango with Nutella Sauce (196)

Harlequin Salad (50)
Turkey Scaloppine with Dried Morels (102)
Middle Eastern Couscous with Saffron (152)
Skillet Apple Charlotte (174)

AUTHOR'S ACKNOWLEDGMENTS

The production of this cookbook and its companion PBS series required the combined efforts of many capable people. Although I can't thank everyone involved in these projects, I would like to mention the names of a few of those whose assistance was invaluable.

The book always comes before the series and wouldn't have been possible without the help of my wife, Gloria, who makes suggestions and advises me in this process. Certainly, too, I want to thank my assistant, Norma Galehouse. This is the twentieth book we've worked on together, and I continue to rely on her ability to transform my handwritten recipes into a workable manuscript.

Thank you to Doe Coover, my agent, who always manages to find the right publisher for my books.

I want to thank Rux Martin at Houghton Mifflin, the editor of this book. Her enthusiasm and guidance helped me with the project and made it interesting and fun. Thanks, also, to the copy editor, Jessica Sherman, whose attention to detail is so important in the publishing process, and to Michaela Sullivan, who was responsible for the book's attractive jacket, and to Ralph Fowler, who did a great job on its interior design, and to Jacinta Monniere, for manuscript preparation.

I am indebted to Tom Hopkins for his extraordinary photography and for being so much fun and so easy to work with. His sharp, clear pictures of my dishes make them look truly good enough to eat. Thanks, too, to Tom's digital technician, Rich Kosenski, and to Marty Travis, a good friend who offered to help style the dishes and who smiled and made us feel good.

More than anyone else, I want to thank my best friend, Jean-Claude Szurdak, who spent a week with me helping with marketing, preparing the food, and organizing ingredients for the photography sessions. His help was precious: I couldn't have done it without him. I am grateful for his friendship and talent.

The television series based on this book is the eleventh of my series filmed at KQED-TV in San Francisco. It required the cooperation of many, many people, and my thanks go out particularly to Jeff Clarke, the president and CEO, who always supports my projects with enthusiasm and kindness. My thanks, too, to Michael Isip, executive producer of the series and vice president for television content and education network. He eagerly supports my vision of fast food, inviting me into his home and his life from the beginning to the end of the project.

I want to thank my cohost on a few of the shows, my daughter, Claudine. It was a great joy to cook with her again and to enjoy her smile and her love.

More than anyone else, I am indebted to Tina Salter, my producer, for her very hard work, dedication, her insights into the project, her thoroughness, and her relaxing demeanor. She dealt with all of the complexities of this production and solved all of the problems with good humor and professionalism. Thanks so much, too, to the director, Marti Hanzlik. She got some incredible close-ups of the food and made me look better as well. I'm grateful to Christine Swett, an associate producer, so kind, gifted, and competent, and to Carol Gancia, also an associate producer, for being always ready with coffee or with any help I needed. Thanks, too, to Elizabeth Pepin, my "cousin," another associate producer, who not only organized all the wine, but drove me around in her car and catered to me with her gentle humor.

I'm grateful to Jolee Hoyt, senior unit manager, for her financial knowledge and for keeping us on track, and to Jenny Zielon, the makeup artist, for making me look better day after day during the three weeks of filming. Thanks, too, to Teresa Morisco, the clothes stylist, and to Andrea Pannes, the prop stylist for the show, as well as Tom Lattanand, the music composer, and Wendy Goodfriend, the Web producer. The series wouldn't have been possible without the hard work of Jacqueline Murray, national marketing director, and Janet Lim Young, director of marketing and corporate events for KQED; they are in charge of raising the money to produce the series and without them I would never be able to tape another show.

Thanks for the expertise of the operations/technical crew, who did a splendid job. This group included Jean Tuckerman and Randy Brase, stage managers; cameramen Harry Betancourt, Mike Elwell, Greg King, and Greg Overton; Eric Shackelford, engineering supervisor; Rick Santangelo, technical director; and Jim McKee, lighting director. This series wouldn't have been possible without their expertise.

Of course, to me, one of the most important aspects of the production is the cooperation and support I get from my fellow cooks in the back kitchen. They are in great part responsible for the quality and success of the shows. First and foremost, my thanks go to David Shalleck, the series' culinary producer, with whom I have worked on many shows and who does a great job organizing the back kitchen staff. Thank you to Laura Pauli, who came from Paris again to choose the dishes for plating my food and also photographed all the finished dishes and organized them so I could have a record of what we had done.

Many thanks, too, to the kitchen staffers, Jacqueline Schwartz and Doug Whitlow, for their hard work. I am truly grateful, also, to the kitchen volunteers: Mike Pleiss, a chemist by profession, who smiles and has helped in the kitchen at each series filming for the past twenty years or so; Stephanie Lucianovic, who made great bread; and Gerald San Jose, formerly of the French Culinary Institute, who volunteered to help in the kitchen.

Again, thanks to everyone involved in the book and the series. Your hard work, cooperation, and dedication made me look good.

PRODUCER'S

ACKNOWLEDGMENTS

Working with Jacques Pépin is a dream. I count myself as very lucky to have my dream come true for the sixth time.

Jacques is the consummate professional. He is amazing. When we roll tape, he cooks. There are no retakes—what you see on your television set at home is Jacques just as he is in the kitchen. His ease in culinary surroundings and his comfort with each technique still surprise me. And, when you taste the food . . .

Taping days begin with Jacques sipping his morning decaf coffee in the back kitchen while checking with David and his crew on the preparation of ingredients for the day's three shows. From there, it's off to makeup and wardrobe. I review the show details with Jacques, often while he's sitting in the makeup chair. In the studio, the team of thirty awaits his arrival, and a new show begins.

To produce twenty-six shows in three weeks takes more than dreams—it's a lot of hard work from a talented, professional, and dedicated team. I would like to thank all the members who have contributed so much to the series: Aaron Drury, the off-line editor, and Robert O'Geen, the online editor; Zaldy Serrano and Carlos Flores, for graphic design; and our hardworking interns, Raquel Arellano, Jessica Mathies, and Tabitha Wong. In operations, Frank Carfi and Kim McCalla made sure that each day ran smoothly. Each member of the team contributes to make every show possible.

We would not be here at all without our funders, and we are very grateful for their generosity. Thank you to . . .

Cuisinart

Cuisinart, Inc.

www.cuisinart.com

 **GOOD GRIPS**

OXO International, Inc.

www.oxo.com

 SCHARFFEN BERGER

Scharffen Berger
Chocolate Maker

www.scharffenberger.com

Spectrum
THE TASTE OF GOODNESS™

Spectrum Organic
Products, Inc.

www.spectrumorganics.com

Thanks must also go to the Prescott Hotel, whose lavish accommodations made Jacques feel comfortable and ready to face each day. This is Jacques's requested home-away-from-home in the Bay Area.

On the set you will see the latest equipment and beautiful props supplied by individuals and companies to make it look like the ideal home kitchen everyone would want. We give special thanks to

BIA Cordon Bleu
Philippe Deshoulieres
www.biacordonbleu.com

John Boos & Co.
www.johnboos.com

Chef'sChoice® by EdgeCraft
EdgeCraft Corp.
www.chefschoice.com

Chef's Warehouse
www.biaoutlet.com

County Restaurant Supply
True Refrigeration
www.crscatalog.com
www.truemfg.com

Emile Henry
www.emilehenryusa.com

J.K. Adams Co.
www.jkadams.com

Kuhn Rikon
www.kuhnrikon.com

LamsonSharp
www.lamsonsharp.com

Le Creuset of America
www.lecreuset.com

MAC Knife, Inc.
www.macknife.com

Mauviel
www.mauviel.com

Microplane
www.microplane.com

PepperMate
www.peppermate.com

Staub
www.staubusa.com

Swissmar and Peugeot
www.swissmar.com

Tokyo Fish Market & Gift Shop

William Bounds
www.wmboundsltd.com

Wüsthof
www.wusthof.com

We also thank

Angray Fantastico
www.fantasticosf.com

The Blue Dog from Venice Clay
www.veniceclay.com

The Butler and & the Chef
Antiques
www.thebutlerandthechef.com

Crate and Barrel
www.crateandbarrel.com

Dover Metals
www.dovermetals.com

Ellington & French
www.ellingtonandfrench.com

Palecek
www.palecek.com

Soule Studio
www.soulestudio.com

Smith & Hawken
www.smithandhawken.com

Sunrise Home
www.sunrisehome.com

A cooking show couldn't manage without ingredients. Some of the freshest and the best were donated by

The Acme Bread Co.
www.acmebread.com

California Caviar Co.
www.californiacaviar.com

Clover Stornetta Farms, Inc.
www.cloverstornetta.com

Consorzio del Formaggio
Parmigiano-Reggiano
www.parmigiano-reggiano.it

Diamond Foods, Inc.
www.diamondnuts.com

Monterey Fish Market
www.montereyfish.com

Egg Innovations
www.egginnovations.com

Nielsen-Massey Vanillas
www.nielsenmassey.com

EO Products
www.eoproducts.com

Niman Ranch
www.nimanranch.com

FAGE USA
www.fageusa.com

Organic Style
www.organicstyle.com

FoodMatch, Inc.
www.foodmatch.com

Pacific Gourmet, Inc.
www.pacgourmet.com

Jeremiah's Pick Coffee Co.
www.jeremiahspick.com

Peet's Coffee & Tea
www.peets.com

GreenLeaf Produce
www.greenleafsf.com

Safeway
www.safeway.com

INDIA TREE – Gourmet Spices
and Specialties
www.indiatree.com

Smart & Final
www.smartandfinal.com

Straus Family Creamery
www.strausfamilycreamery.com

McEvoy Ranch
www.mcevoyranch.com

Vanilla, Saffron Imports
www.saffron.com

Modesto Food Distributors, Inc.
www.modestofood.com

For Jacques, food and wine are inseparable. Some of the very best
beverages were donated by

KQED Wine Club
www.kqedwineclub.org

Anchor Brewing Company
www.anchorbrewing.com

A Donkey and Goat Winery
www.adonkeyandgoat.com

Broadbent Selections
www.broadbent.com

Broc Cellars
www.broccellars.com

Kuleto Estate Winery
www.kuletoestate.com

Craft Distillers/Germain-Robin
www.craftdistillers.com

Moët & Chandon
www.moet.com

Department C Wines
www.deptcwines.com

Pacific Rim Winemakers
www.pacificrimwinemakers.com

Duckhorn Wine Company
www.duckhorn.com

Pepin Vineyard
www.pepinvineyard.com

Frei Brothers
www.freibrothers.com

Pernod Ricard USA
www.pernod-ricard-usa.com

Judd's Hill Winery
www.juddshill.com

St. Supéry Vineyards and Winery
www.stsupery.com

Kendric Vineyards
www.kendricvineyards.com

Stag's Leap Wine Cellars
www.cask23.com

—Tina Salter, Producer

INDEX

pork *(continued)*
   tenderloin, stuffed, on grape tomatoes, *112,* 113–14
potato(es)
   criques (potato pancakes) on mesclun salad, 144–46, *145*
   gnocchi with eggs and scallions, 44, *45*
   gratin with cream, 143
   mashed, fluffy, 142
poultry. *See* chicken; turkey
pressure cookers, about, 119
prosciutto or serrano ham and tomato bread, Spanish, *6, 7*
pudding, tapioca banana coconut, 197
pumpkin gratin, 138

Q

quick lamb stew, 115–17, *116*

R

radish toasts, *6, 7*
ragout of broccolini, beans, and sausage, 134
raisins
   rice with, 147
   spinach, and macadamia nuts, 135, *135*
raspberry(ies)
   peach Melba, 186, *187*
   sauce, mini almond cakes in, 208, *209*
   small berry custards, *176,* 177
   tart, cookie dough, 210–11, *211*
ratatouille with penne, *155,* 155–56
rice
   picante mussel pilaf, 64–65, *65*
   with raisins, 147
   risotto with broccoli stems, 148–50, *149*
   shellfish and chicken paella, 89–91, *90*
rice paper rolls with avocado and sun-dried tomato, *xiv,* 22
ricotta gâteaux, sweet, with peach sauce, *188,* 189
rigatoni with lettuce and eggplant, 160, *161*
risotto with broccoli stems, 148–50, *149*
roasted split chicken with mustard crust, 99–101, *100*

rochers, chocolate, with hazelnuts and cornflakes, 212–13, *213*
romesco sauce, 78

S

salads
   asparagus fans with mustard sauce, *48,* 49
   beet, Stilton, apple, and nut, 4
   crabmeat horseradish, 4
   cured herring starter, 5
   frisée aux lardons (curly endive with bacon bits), 53–55, *54*
   Greek tomato, tall, *47,* 52
   harlequin, 50, *51*
   surimi, on greens, 16
   tomato surprise, 56–57, *57*
salmon
   burgers on baby arugula, 84
   cured, morsels, 12, *13*
   mousse, 18, *19*
   poached, in sour cream–herb sauce, 83
   rolls, 18, *19*
   smoked, pizza, 164, *165*
sandwiches
   mini croques-monsieur, 8, *9*
sauces
   horseradish, red, 74–75, *75*
   horseradish, white, 74–75, *75*
   lemon-butter, 86–88
   lemon–olive oil, 86–88
   mustard, *48,* 49
   pimiento, 79
   romesco, 78
   yogurt-cucumber, 120
sausage(s)
   bits, glazed, *20,* 21
   broccolini, and beans, ragout of, 134
   chorizo, mushroom, and cheese pizza, 163
   hot, sautéed curly mustard greens with, 126, *127*
   patties with pumpkin seeds and mushrooms, *108,* 109
sautéed curly mustard greens with hot sausage, 126, *127*
sautéed julienned endive, 125
sautéed stuffed figs with blueberries, 194
savory iceberg cups, *10,* 11

sautéed stuffed figs with blueberries, 194

tomato surprise, 56–57, *57*

Y

yogurt

-cucumber sauce, 120

Greek, walnuts, and honey, *206,* 207

Z

zucchini

poached salmon in sour cream–herb sauce, 83

ratatouille with penne, *155,* 155–56

salmon rolls, 18, *19*

tomato surprise, 56–57, *57*